access to

RUSSIA 1815–81

Second Edition

Russell Sherman
and Robert Pearce

Hodder Murray

MEMBER OF THE HODDER HEADLINE GROUP

Acknowledgements

The front cover illustration shows Tsar Alexander I (courtesy of the Royal Society of Medicine).

The publishers would like to thank the following for permission to reproduce copyright illustrations in this book:

The Hulton Getty Picture Collection, pages 57 & 122 and the David King Collection, page 94.

Orders: please contact Bookpoint Ltd, 130 Milton Park, Abingdon, Oxon OX14 4SB. Telephone (44) 01235 827720, Fax: (44) 01235 400454. Lines are open from 9.00–6.00, Monday to Saturday, with a 24 hour message answering service. You can also order through our website **www.hoddereducation.co.uk**

British Library Cataloguing in Publication Data
A catalogue record for this title is available from the British Library

ISBN-10: 0 340 75840 6
ISBN-13: 978 0 340 75840 3

First published 2002
Impression number   10 9 8 7 6 5 4 3
Year   2008 2007 2006 2005

Typeset by Fakenham Photosetting limited, Fakenham, Norfork
Printed in Great Britain for Hodder Murray, an imprint of Hodder Education, a member of the Hodder Headline Group, 338 Euston Road, London NW1 3BH by CPI Bath

Contents

Preface

To the general reader

Although the *Access to History* series has been designed with the needs of students studying the subject at higher examination levels very much in mind, it also has a great deal to offer the general reader. The main body of the text (i.e. ignoring the 'Study Guides' at the ends of chapters) forms a readable and yet stimulating survey of a coherent topic as studied by historians. However, each author's aim has not merely been to provide a clear explanation of what happened in the past (to interest and inform): it has also been assumed that most readers wish to be stimulated into thinking further about the topic and to form opinions of their own about the significance of the events that are described and discussed (to be challenged). Thus, although no prior knowledge of the topic is expected on the reader's part, she or he is treated as an intelligent and thinking person throughout. The author tends to share ideas and possibilities with the reader, rather than passing on numbers of so-called 'historical truths'.

To the student reader

Although advantage has been taken of the publication of a second edition to ensure the results of recent research are reflected in the text, the main alteration from the first edition is the inclusion of new features, and the modification of existing ones, aimed at assisting you in your study of the topic at AS level, A level and Higher. Two features are designed to assist you during your first reading of a chapter. The *Points to Consider* section following each chapter title is intended to focus your attention on the main theme(s) of the chapter, and the issues box following most section headings alerts you to the question or questions to be dealt with in the section. The *Working on...* section at the end of each chapter suggests ways of gaining maximum benefit from the chapter.

There are many ways in which the series can be used by students studying History at a higher level. It will, therefore, be worthwhile thinking about your own study strategy before you start your work on this book. Obviously, your strategy will vary depending on the aim you have in mind, and the time for study that is available to you.

If, for example, you want to acquire a general overview of the topic in the shortest possible time, the following approach will probably be the most effective:

1. Read chapter 1. As you do so, keep in mind the issues raised in the *Points to Consider* section.

2. Read the *Points to Consider* section at the beginning of chapter 2 and decide whether it is necessary for you to read this chapter.
3. If it is, read the chapter, stopping at each heading or sub-heading to note down the main points that have been made. Often, the best way of doing this is to answer the question(s) posed in the Key Issues boxes.
4. Repeat stage 2 (and stage 3 where appropriate) for all the other chapters.

If, however, your aim is to gain a thorough grasp of the topic, taking however much time is necessary to do so, you may benefit from carrying out the same procedure with each chapter, as follows:

1. Try to read the chapter in one sitting. As you do this, bear in mind any advice given in the *Points to Consider* section.
2. Study the flow diagram at the end of the chapter, ensuring that you understand the general 'shape' of what you have just read.
3. Read the *Working on...* section and decide what further work you need to do on the chapter. In particularly important sections of the book, this is likely to involve reading the chapter a second time and stopping at each heading and sub-heading to think about (and probably to write a summary of) what you have just read.
4. Attempt the *Source-based questions* section. It will sometimes be sufficient to think through your answers, but additional understanding will often be gained by forcing yourself to write them down.

When you have finished the main chapters of the book, study the 'Further Reading' section and decide what additional reading (if any) you will do on the topic.

This book has been designed to help make your studies both enjoyable and successful. If you can think of ways in which this could have been done more effectively, please contact us. In the meantime, we hope that you will gain greatly from your study of History.

Keith Randell & Robert Pearce

Russia in 1815

POINTS TO CONSIDER

To understand what took place in nineteenth-century Russia you need to know what made her different – different from other states at the time and different from today. This chapter looks at the geography of Russia, her social and political structures, and at her trade, industry and economy. Nineteenth-century Russia is often seen as one of a number of European states; but this is at least as misleading as looking at contemporary Russia as a western European state today. As you read this chapter you should concentrate on developing a clear picture of these differences.

Russia did not share the same intellectual, religious or social traditions as Western Europe. The Russian Orthodox Church was very different from the Western Christian churches. There was no tradition of the Tsar sharing power with any group. Even the Russian alphabet was distinct and different. Europe was important to Russia, but so were the vast territories to the east. The size of Russia alone distinguished her from her European contemporaries. The map on page 2 was deliberately chosen to show a Russian perspective. It reveals that she was far more than a European power. Russia was a vast sprawling empire made up of numerous nationalities. Her people were as diverse in language and culture as were the lands they inhabited. This disparate empire was held together by the autocratic power of the Tsars rather than by any natural bond between her peoples.

1 Russian Geography

KEY ISSUE How did Russian geography affect what could be achieved, and what was likely to be achieved, in political, economic and social terms?

A grasp of Russian geography is central to an understanding of Russian development. Today, it is rare for expert commentators to make more than a passing reference to the physical and climatic geography of a country. In the developed world at least, science and technology are often seen as being able to overcome the majority of natural problems faced by societies. Before these advances were made, however, geography was often a major factor in determining the nature and scope of human activity. By 1815 Russia covered almost one-sixth of the total land surface of the world. It stretched some 3,000 miles from the frozen wastes of the Arctic in the north to the arid deserts above Afghanistan in the south, and nearly 6,000

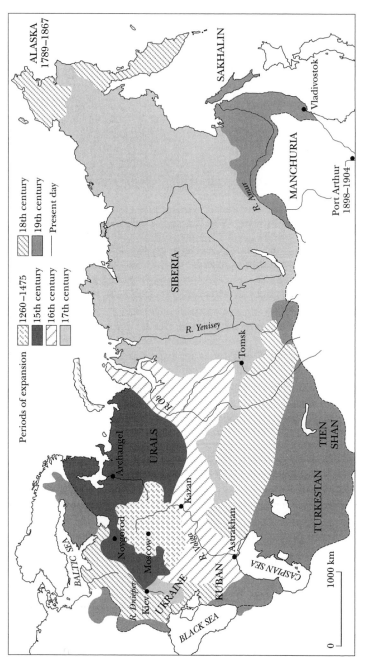

The Expansion of the Russian Empire

miles from central Europe in the west out towards Alaska in the east. The diversity of these regions and the diversity of climate placed severe limitations on Russia's development and growth.

Very little of the land mass that comprised the Russian state was hospitable and productive. Russian vegetation can be divided into four main areas (see the map on page 4). The tundra to the north is too cold to support plant growth or unassisted human activity; the great forest zone, the taiga (swampy coniferous forest) and wooded forest, is the largest forested area in the world; the steppe is a vast grassland plain which stretches from Hungary to Mongolia; and the semi-desert regions of Central Asia are unable to support large numbers of people.

There are two main areas fit for human habitation: the steppe and the southern part of the forest region. These were described by Baron Haxthausen in the 1840s:

1 In the north of Russia the vegetation springs up into a forest; every fallow field, every uncultivated spot is covered with wood in a few years ... In the Steppes, nature shoots up into grass and flowers; and what a luxuriant growth! Plants which are at most two feet tall with us, here rise
5 higher than the head.

This appears to paint a picture of a rich and fertile land ready to be exploited. Owing to the nature of both soil and climate, however, this is misleading. Russia has a 'continental' climate, hot in summer but very cold in winter. The further east one progresses, the colder the winter becomes. Temperatures at Verkhoyansk in eastern Siberia fall to $-50°$ C in January. Much of eastern Siberia, although on the same latitude as England, is impossible to cultivate. In the remainder the growing season is very short. Agricultural effort has to be concentrated into a very brief period in these areas. In the north of European Russia, which forms the core of the old Russian state, the land stays frozen for up to eight months a year. This factor, combined with uneven rainfall, led to one harvest in three being barely able to support the population. Rainfall is low in the most fertile areas of the black earth belt, but quite high in the sandy, less fertile soils to the north-west. Yet even here the rainfall is concentrated into the last two months of the growing season, so that it only has to be a few weeks late to cause severe problems.

The result of these adverse conditions was low crop yields. By 1820 Russian wheat yields averaged 1:3 (three grains gathered for every one planted). In central Europe they averaged over 1:5, while in England they had already reached 1:8. This meant that the Russian peasant had very little surplus to meet the needs of a bad year, to eat, to sell or to feed animals through the long winters. This in turn meant that there was little manure available to put life back into the soil, especially in the north where it was most needed.

Such poor yields cannot be blamed entirely on the adverse factors

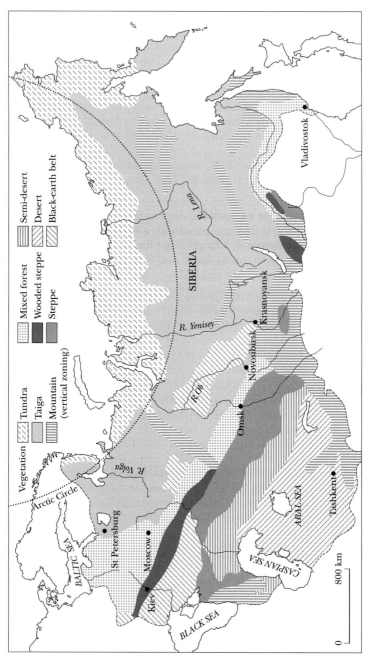

The Russian Empire – vegetation and soil type

described above. In western Europe the growth of trade and cities had gone hand in hand with improvements in agriculture, one stimulating and reinforcing the other, providing the incentive for increased production. In Russia that incentive was lacking. The social and economic system did not allow the peasantry to reap the benefits of any increases in productivity. The limited progress, which was made, was more than swallowed up by the rapid increase in population that took place after 1750 (see the graph below). This population increase, coupled with the fact that the lack of an effective source of fertilizer meant that the fertility of land in the north was regularly exhausted, led to a continued expansion into new, still fertile, areas.

2 Social Structure

> **KEY ISSUE** How did the way in which Russian society was organised affect and limit the ways in which Russia was likely to develop in political and economic terms?

Russia was a rural state. About 96 per cent of the population lived in the countryside. The vast majority were peasants. The old social unit in Russia had been based on the extended family group, often numbering up to 50 or more people. By 1815 this had been largely

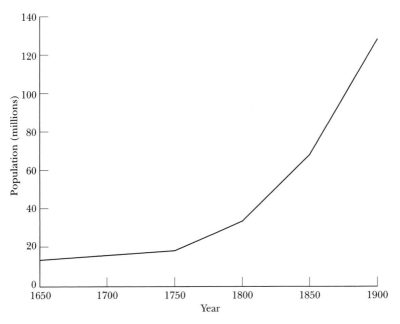

'Russian Population Growth'

replaced by the village commune or *mir*. Most villages were made up of a number of smaller extended families and had fewer than 500 inhabitants. Decision-making, binding on the whole village, was carried out by a group made up of the heads of families. This appears to have suited the landlords, the peasants and the circumstances of the time. Landlords found it easier to deal with one representative of an extended family, rather than the individual members. The *mir* council also acted as a self-regulating body, which took the administrative burden away from the landlord, dealing with the vexed question of allotting land to members of the commune and administering taxes and rents. The *mir* also seems to have given the majority of peasants a feeling of security, which they desired. The communal nature of the organisation suited the situation. The short growing season demanded bursts of intense, coordinated activity, while the shortage of fertile land made such cooperation and coordination even more important if the peasants were to squeeze enough from the land to survive.

There were two main categories of peasant: the serfs, who were privately owned; and the state peasants, who lived on land that had not been given to private ownership and were therefore owned by the state. The serfs were the property of their owner and could be bought and sold, made to work where the owner wished and had virtually no effective legal rights. Although the lives of the serfs, and those of the state peasants, were often hard and unrewarding, comparisons with the slave plantations of America, or even the collective farms of Stalin's era, are misleading. As will be discussed later (see page 57), there were many moral and economic arguments against the system, but the peasants were generally free to keep the profits of their labour, if they could make any, over and above the demands of their landlord or the state. These demands were growing as the landowning class increasingly fell into debt, but economic expediency, coupled with the inefficiency of the system, prevented the majority of landlords from placing impossible demands on their serfs.

The peasants lived an alternately rigorous and monotonous life, but their existence was comparable to that of peasants in any pre-industrial society. The fact that this system of serfdom still existed up until 1861 is vital in understanding Russia's development. Serfdom began to die out in Western Europe from the end of the thirteenth century. Even in the Austrian Empire it had been abolished by the end of the eighteenth. In Russia it remained as a block to individual innovation and enterprise and to economic development and industrialisation.

The peasantry made up about 83 per cent of the population. What of the remainder? The most accurate figures for the period come from Arsenev, a statistician who produced the following table, which divided Russia's population into two groups, productive and unproductive. This table raises the importance at the time of various *legal* definitions of class, which formed important barriers between the classes.

Arsenev's Table of Classes -	Based on the censuses of 1812 and 1816	
Unproductive Classes	**Thousands**	**Percentage**
Nobility	450	1.1
Clergy	430	1.1
Military	2,000	5.0
Officials and *Raznochinsty*	1,500	3.7
Total	4,380	10.9
Productive Classes		
Merchants	204	0.5
Meshchanin	1,490	3.7
State Peasants	13,100	32.7
Serfs	20,300	50.7
'Free people'	234	0.6
Other peasants	360	0.9
Total	35,688	89.1
Unproductive + Productive	40,068	100

The most important aspect of this table is that it shows that there was a very small 'middle class'. This 'middle class' was strictly controlled. *Meshchanin* was a legal term that covered a variety of the poorer town-dwellers such as labourers, artisans and small shopkeepers. They could engage in business, but only within strictly defined limits on what and how much they could buy and sell. If they were particularly successful, they could try to join one of the merchant guilds. This involved the payment of an entry fee as well as a legal change of status. Even when the money for this could be raised, the authorities frequently did not allow this change of status to take place. Even if a member of the *Meshchanin* gained the rights of a merchant, he still had to work within the strict rules laid down by the state for the guild he joined. Movement between classes was difficult at any level, but as a rule the lower down the scale you were, the more difficult it was. This limited enterprise, initiative and motivation. However, even serfs were theoretically able to, and sometimes did, buy their freedom.

The *Raznochintsy* were a mixed group. They were relatively well-educated people, but because they were not nobles and were only of low *rank*, they did not easily fit into normal classifications. They were important for two main reasons. They provided the basis of the Russian intelligentsia, which in turn provided many of the leaders of the Russian revolutionary movements in the 19th century. They also brought to the fore the problems of the system of 'ranks' The 'Table of Ranks' (see page 10) was inextricably linked to the nature and form of the Russian autocracy. It demonstrated and characterised the hierarchical nature of Russian society. Everyone had a place and station in life, and it was very difficult to alter that place and station. This also naturally tended to stifle ambition, enterprise and initiative.

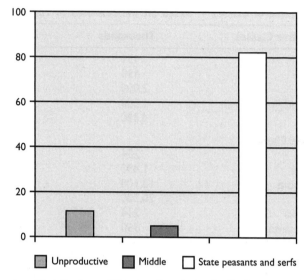

Percentage Distribution of Russian Population by Socio-economic Class, circa 1815

3 The Autocracy

Autocracy in Russia was autocracy in perhaps its purest form. All policy and decision-making lay in the hands of the Tsar. The Tsar expected, and for the most part received, the willing and total sub-

> **KEY ISSUE** How did the autocratic political structures affect and limit the ways in which Russia was likely to develop in political and economic terms?

mission of his subjects. All his subjects were theoretically equal before him. His task was to be the strong 'father', who loved all his 'children' equally, who punished them when necessary, who kept order and who protected the fatherland from external threat. In turn, the Tsar was subject to God, and was responsible to Him for the spiritual and physical well-being of the people.

Some may feel that distinct similarities and parallels exist between this type of ruler and the 'Divine Right' monarchs of Western Europe. However, this is a misleading comparison, with the possible exception of Spain in an earlier period. In Russia the autocrat had virtually never shared power with other groups. The great majority of Russians believed this was as it should be. They felt that the sharing of power would lead to corruption and the growth of privileged groups. They regarded the idea of privilege as inherently evil, something which would lead to weakness and misery for all. Until as recently as the later nineteenth century, many strong critics of the regime did not question the *idea* of autocracy, but rather focused on corrupt or inefficient officials or landlords. Even the serfs tended to see the Tsar as their 'little father', who was merely misled by his advisers.

Why was the autocracy seen in this light? The size, nature and scope of the Russian Empire provide part of the answer. The task of ruling and defending such a vast and sprawling country, which possessed no effective natural defences, was not an easy one. It was made up of numerous nationalities, such as the Ukrainians and Lithuanians in the west, the Georgians and Cossacks in the south, and the Uzbeks and Tartars in the east. Russia needed strong government. The danger of invasion seemed always to be present. Also the Tsar's armies had been responsible for Russia's expansion and were therefore seen as closely linked to Russia's power and prestige.

At the same time, Russian government required a complex hierarchy. The land was divided into provinces, which were sub-divided into districts, and further divided down to the village. This was because communications were so slow that the vast distances involved required the Tsar's representatives in the far-flung outposts of the Empire, at whatever level, to wield power for him. This had two major effects. Firstly it made the Tsar remote from his people, and often led them to blame his representatives, rather than the Tsar himself, for their problems. Secondly, the very complexity of the hierarchy acted as a brake on innovation and progress.

The Orthodox Church, which saw the Tsar as an emperor (*autokrator*), provides another part of the answer. Higher ranking clergy, the black clergy (so called because of their black robes), were supported financially by the state and largely appointed from the upper classes. It was, to a large extent, an unworldly Church. Its main emphasis was on ritual and on the next world, as opposed to the passing vagaries of this. But it actively supported a succession of Tsars as the rightful rulers of the country and thus provided a firm theological basis for the Tsarist autocracy. So, whilst the Orthodox Church did not take an active part in political affairs (largely because it did not see this world as being of great importance), it did have a major impact on how the Tsars were seen by the Russian people. If religion ever was the 'opium of the people', it was so in Russia more than in any other country. The impact of a peasant based society, with limited economic opportunities, where very few people were educated and where communication of ideas was both limited and controlled, completes the picture. A tradition of feeling under threat, where success had apparently come because of autocratic power, where economic, social and cultural horizons were very restricted and where the Tsar was supported by God and the Church in an often harsh climate led to an unquestioning and often fond acceptance of the Tsar's rule. Periodic peasant revolts rarely focused on the Tsar or his position. They targeted his corrupt or inept servants.

The bureaucratic nature of Russian society had been formally categorised by Peter the Great in 1722 when he published the 'Table of Ranks'. This was part of his plan for restructuring the Russian state. The table divided the ruling class into 14 ranks. Each member of the nobility had to serve the Tsar for his whole life, either in military or civil service. In theory at least, each noble had to start at the lowest rank and work his way up the ladder. The top eight ranks brought hereditary nobility, whilst the lowest six ranks brought personal nobility. Nobles owed their position to their service of the Tsar. This was the opposite of the old *Boyar* (the traditional Russian noble) idea of inherent nobility. The original system of ranks set up by Peter the Great depended on lifelong service and the idea of promotion on merit.

By 1815, however, promotion was already more often determined by length of service than by ability, and lifelong service was no longer compulsory. Without these elements, the system of ranks ceased to be a positive factor and instead became a stultifying force, which militated against change, initiative and efficiency.

The Table of Ranks

Rank	Military	Civil
1	Field Marshal	Chancellor
2	General	Active Privy Councillor
3	Lieutenant General	Procurator General
4	Major General	Privy Councillor
5	Brigadier	Civil Councillor
6	Colonel	Superior Court President
7	Lieutenant Colonel	Aulic Councillor
8	Captain	Collegial Assessor
9	First Lieutenant	Titular Councillor
10	Second Lieutenant	College Secretary
11	–	Ship's Secretary
12	Sub-Lieutenant	Provincial Secretary
13	Ensign 1st Class	Senate Registrar
14	Ensign 2nd Class	College Registrar

Many of the terms used above will be unfamiliar. A detailed knowledge of what they mean is not needed to see just how stratified the 'Table' was, and how easily such a system could become a negative force once the basis of promotion ceased to be merit and ability and became replaced by influence and length of service.

4 Trade, Industry and the Economy

> **KEY ISSUE** How did the way in which the economy and industry were organised affect and limit the ways in which Russia was likely to develop in political and social terms?

The Russian economy is often dismissed as backward and underdeveloped at this time. This is a dangerous over-simplification. The Russian economy was neither static nor insignificant. It was developing, although at a much slower rate than economies in most other parts of Europe.

At the beginning of the nineteenth century, Russian iron smelting accounted for one-third of the world's iron production and Russia exported over 50,000 tons a year, mainly to England. Iron production grew by over 50 per cent in the first half of the nineteenth century. This might appear to be an impressive rate of growth, but it was not. In 1800 Russian iron production was roughly the equivalent of English iron production. Yet by 1850, England produced 12 times as much iron as Russia. This relative stagnation was the result of Russian iron becoming too expensive to sell in European markets. It was expensive partly because of the very high cost of transporting it from the distant Urals (the centre of the Russian iron industry), and partly because investment and modernisation did not take place in Russia as it did elsewhere. This was to some extent due to the government's policy of protecting Russian industry from foreign competition. Protection, coupled with the use of serf labour, meant that Russian industrialists did not perceive the need to institute significant change. The obvious economic benefits of change, present elsewhere in Europe, were lacking. Similarly, many of the factors normally seen as necessary for rapid industrial expansion – available capital, administrative flexibility and an established entrepreneurial class – were absent. The woolen, coal and chemical industries suffered similar relative stagnation.

There was one area of significant progress during the first half of the nineteenth century. This was the cotton industry. It developed rapidly, using technology brought from England. The Russian cotton industry was able to expand firstly because the Napoleonic wars protected the home industry from English competition, and further high tariffs were erected after 1822. Secondly, after 1815, it was able to buy cheap yarn and later cheap spinning machines from England, because it suited the English to allow them to do so. Finally it benefited from being a new industry, which therefore suffered less from traditional restrictions. By 1850, the Russian cotton industry had become the fifth largest in the world. Even then, however, total production was not much above 10 per cent of English production.

Nevertheless, as an examination of the figures given below will show, there was real progress in absolute terms. The lack of growth in the Russian economy was relative and not absolute. It was only in relation to other, far more active economies, that Russia was stagnating.

The nature of the Russian state was largely responsible for this relative stagnation. Trade and industry took place in the traditional way, largely by means of the royal appointment of monopolies. A competitive business economy had not yet developed. Most domestic trade was carried out through the antiquated system of fairs (large markets – often yearly), which were still responsible for the majority of internal trade until the 1860s. Both the state and private banking systems were weak and unstable, and money was scarce and subject to severe fluctuations in value. It was still very difficult to invest in companies and therefore to find capital for expansion and development. Joint stock companies only began to appear at the beginning of the nineteenth century, and even then they were severely restricted by state legislation until the latter half of the century. Thus the atmosphere, the freedom and the infrastructure, which encouraged rapid economic growth in Western Europe and America, simply did not exist in Russia at this time, and the thrusting middle class, which drove industrialisation forward in Western Europe, was not present.

Production Figures

Product	Year	Total Production by value in Roubles
Cotton	1814	32,000
Cotton	1852	1,835,000
Wool	1815	785,000
Wool	1852	29,077,000

Total exports rose on average by a factor of 10, in the period 1802–60.

Exports by value (in roubles)

Product	1802	1860
Wheat	1,158,000	37,508,000
Rye	1,600,000	12,117,000
Fat & Lard	2,752,000	18,221,000
Furs	720,000	2,394,000
Wool	275,000	19,748,000
Metals and other products	1,370,000	2,569,000

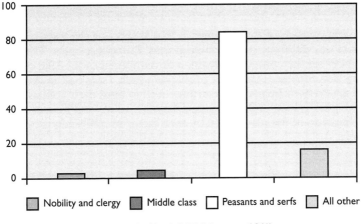

Economic/Social Divisions, c. 1815

Summary Diagram
Summary – Russia in 1815

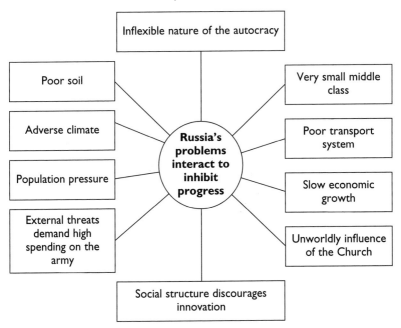

Working on Chapter 1

The importance of this Chapter is that it sets out the ways in which Russia was different from contemporary European states. These differences set the context for Russian development in the 19th century. They also represent the basic problems which Tsars had to deal with, and which both helped to determine and to limit their actions. It will be helpful to look at the summary diagram above and to write a brief explanation of the part played by each factor in inhibiting progress in Russia.

Source-based questions on Chapter 1

1. Russian Geography

Carefully study the maps on pages 2 and 4, and the population graph on page 5. Then answer the following questions:

a) What does the second map show about the relationship in size and geography between Russia and Europe? (*2 marks*)
b) Why is the perspective so different from what you are used to? Does this mean that it is misleading? (*5 marks*)
c) What implications did the situation portrayed in the population graph have for Russian agriculture and administration in the nineteenth century? (*5 marks*)
d) What problems does the first map suggest this rise in population will cause? (*3 marks*)

2. The Economy

Carefully study the production and export figures given on page 12.

a) Draw a graph to show the percentage increase in cotton and wool production. (*7 marks*)
b) Describe what these graphs indicate about the comparative rate of growth of these industries. (*3 marks*)
c) Explain what these figures might suggest about the growth of the Russian machine industry. (*3 marks*)
d) Do the export and production figures give different pictures of the Russian economy? Explain any differences you find. What disadvantages are there in a country relying on primary products as its main exports? (*7 marks*)

2 Alexander I 1801–25

POINTS TO CONSIDER

Tsar Alexander I remains something of an enigma. He made many statements suggesting he was in favour of reform, particularly in terms of a constitution and emancipation of the serfs. At times his actions suggested that he would carry through significant changes. Yet in the end he did not manage to do so. This leaves us with two key questions. Was he committed to reform? If so, what prevented him from carrying it through, personal weaknesses or forces beyond his control? As you read through this chapter you should concentrate on these two issues.

KEY DATES

1801	Murder of Paul I; accession of Alexander.
1802	Abolition of Secret Police; hopes raised for liberalisation.
1805	Russia declares war on France but loses Battle of Austerlitz.
1807	Treaty of Tilsit (alliance between Russia and France). Speransky appointed as special adviser.
1809	Speransky finishes draft constitution, which was accepted in principle but little implemented.
1812	Speransky dismisses nobility. France invades Russia.
1815	Napoleon finally defeated; Peace Settlement.
1816	Foundation of first revolutionary societies. Emancipation of Estonian serfs raises hopes of change in Russia. Military Colonies expanded under Arakcheyev.
1817	Arakcheyev appointed chief advisor, a reactionary influence. Golitsyn appointed Minster of education, a liberal influence.
1820	2nd draft constitution presented to Alexander. Rebellion of St Petersburg regiments shocks Alexander; draft constitutions rejected.
1822	Edict dissolves all secret societies – repression.
1825	Death of Alexander I.

1 Alexander the Man

> **KEY ISSUE** How did his early life impact on his character and beliefs?

His critics see Alexander as secretive, introspective, hypocritical and deceitful. His reign has often been characterised as a period of liberal intent followed by a period of severe repression. Whilst these comments contain an element of truth, they show only one side of the complex nature of both the man and his reign.

Alexander was born in 1777. He was the eldest son of the heir to the throne, Paul. But he was taken from his parents by his grandmother the Empress Catherine. She took charge of his education and was determined that he should be groomed to be the ideal ruler of the future. She picked his tutors herself and personally wrote a number of texts for her grandson to study. Surprisingly, the most prominent of his tutors, La Harpe, was a Swiss and was both a republican and a democrat. La Harpe was Alexander's main intellectual guide from the age of seven to 17, and Alexander was imbued at this early age with a respect and admiration for the ideas of liberty and equality that his tutor held.

When he was with his father, Alexander was exposed to a completely different regime. His father spent most of his time at his isolated residence of Gatchina, where he occupied himself by repeatedly drilling his small honour guard. Paul encouraged Alexander to become the perfect modern soldier, which for Paul meant strict discipline and regimentation on the Prussian model. Although this was something of a contrast to the spoiled existence Alexander enjoyed at his grandmother's court, he did seem to develop a real liking for the precision and order he found at Gatchina. Yet relations between father and son were far from easy, and it is not surprising that the young Alexander became somewhat introspective and secretive, given the stark contrasts to which he was exposed and the need to please the very different demands of his father and grandmother.

Catherine died in 1796 and Paul came to the throne. In 1801 a group of officers planned to remove Paul, whom they rightly saw as unpredictable and ineffectual, and to place Alexander on the throne. They told Alexander of their plan, and he acquiesced on the condition that they would spare his father's life. They agreed to these conditions, but then murdered Paul anyway. This involvement in his father's murder, although unintentional, led to feelings of guilt on Alexander's part that were to have a profound effect on him, particularly in later years.

Alexander, in a letter to his tutor in late 1797, outlined his criticisms of his father and his future hopes, and in many ways he described some of the criticisms which would later be leveled at himself.

> 1 My father ... wished to reform everything. The beginning ... was sparkling enough but what followed did not fulfill expectations. Everything has been turned upside down at once ... he has no plan to follow; he orders today what a month later he countermands ... If ever
> 5 the time comes for me to rule, instead of leaving my country, I should do better to work to make my country free and to preserve it from serving in the future as the plaything of a madman ...

2 The Early Years 1801–15

> **KEY ISSUE** How far should the first period of Alexander's reign be seen as liberal?

Alexander's reign began with a distinctly liberal flourish. The year 1801 saw the repeal of almost all the harsh and oppressive legislation passed by Paul. Those who had been arrested were freed, those who had been exiled were allowed to return, and the use of torture was forbidden. Alexander wished that 'the very name of torture, the shame and reproach of humanity, will be wiped forever from the memory of the nation'. In 1802 the secret police were abolished. He attempted to establish a clear and fair legal system to replace the chaos of the existing one. Unfortunately, the commission which he set up to codify the law did not possess the necessary vision or strength to overcome the problems it faced. The new Tsar surrounded himself with young and forward-looking advisers – a group known by its supporters as 'the committee of public salvation' and by its critics as the 'Jacobin Gang' (a reference to the most famous egalitarian political group in the French Revolution – the Jacobins). Both descriptions were exaggerated, but they point clearly to the sharp division that existed between the liberal and conservative elements in Russian society.

Whatever Alexander's faults, significant legislation was passed during this period. The right to own estates was extended to 'free Russians' other than the nobility. In 1803, a law was enacted which allowed for voluntary emancipation of serfs by their masters. Although this measure has frequently been criticised because it did not go far enough, it was significant nevertheless, and by 1850 over 100,000 male serfs had been emancipated with their families under the terms of this legislation. Improving the education system was made a priority. In 1804 an Education Statute was the beginning of a more western approach to education. Several new universities were founded, along with over 40 secondary schools and numerous other schools.

At Alexander's request, the most comprehensive proposal for reform was drawn up by Michael Speransky, who was appointed special advisor in 1807. This was the plan for constitutional reform, which was completed in 1809. This plan envisaged dividing government into three branches: legislature, executive and judiciary. The property-owning classes were to enjoy both civil and political rights, whilst the 'working people' were to enjoy civil rights. Alexander approved this plan in principle. It fitted in with his desire, expressed before his accession, 'to give Russia freedom and so save her from the encroachments of despotism and tyranny'.

As a first step, in 1810, the Council of State was created to advise the Tsar. In an attempt to improve the vague and muddled nature of central government, new ministries were established with specific responsibilities. Clear guidelines were also set out on how they should carry out their duties. Some attempt was made to ensure that promotion in the civil service was once more by merit, rather than by seniority, with the introduction of examinations and qualifications.

These changes were largely organised by Speransky. However, by pushing for both a duma (parliament) and income tax, he provoked such strong opposition from the nobility that Alexander was forced to dismiss him in March 1812. This dismissal illustrates the difference between theory and practice, which characterised so much of Alexander's reign. The Tsar may have ruled supreme, but he still depended on the support of the nobility. The conservative elites in Russia may have shown no real sign of wishing to take power themselves, but they certainly did not wish to give power to others, or to see their own importance diminished.

Similarly Alexander may have taken the almost revolutionary step of personally ordering that the treatise of the English reformer Jeremy Bentham on civil and penal law be translated into Russian, but he could not escape from the fact that he was the Tsar of a country whose people in practice had no civil rights as Bentham conceived them. As Tsar he was entrusted with the welfare of all his people, yet his actions were limited by the power structures of the Russian state and the need to maintain its stability, especially when Russia was threatened from abroad.

Shortly after Speransky's dismissal, as the Tsar had expected, the alliance with France (at the Peace of Tilsit in 1807, following Napoleon's victory over Russia at Austerlitz two years earlier) broke down. Napoleon invaded again. Russia needed unity to face this major threat. Other considerations had to be put aside, especially such potentially divisive ones as reforms which limited the powers of the Tsar and the nobility. For the next three years Alexander concentrated on the defeat of Napoleon and the peace negotiations that followed.

Alexander played a major part in bringing about Napoleon's defeat. He was hailed as the 'hero of liberation', a role that he felt to be justly his. He insisted on taking a personal role in the post-Napoleonic settlement. There seems little doubt that he felt that he had some form of divine mission to accomplish. At the time this mission was apparently quite liberal. He insisted that the restored French monarchy grant a constitution to its people. Although some doubted his motives, he insisted on the formation of a Polish state, with himself at its head. He granted the new state a constitution, which many contemporaries thought remarkably liberal, in that it granted civil rights in Poland, which were not granted in Russia. The religious element came to the fore in the Holy Alliance (see page 105), which embodied Alexander's own personal vision for the future. He exhorted his fellow Christian monarchs to live as brothers and to preserve peace as a holy duty, according to the 'supreme truths dictated by the eternal law of God the Saviour'. Though England refrained from joining the alliance and the British Foreign Minister, Castlereagh, went so far as to call the whole enterprise 'a piece of sublime mysticism and nonsense', all the other Christian heads of state in Europe joined, with the exception of the Pope. Yet it was only Alexander who really seems to have viewed this alliance as part of a 'Holy mission to carry out God's will on earth'.

3 Alexander After 1815

> **KEY ISSUES** Should the second period of his reign be seen as repressive? Are there common threads running through the early and late period of his reign?

The period after 1815 is often seen as a period of Russian reaction, in which the Tsar moved away from his liberal ideas towards brutal repression. This view has some basis in terms of what actually took place, but is a misrepresentation of Alexander's intent.

Perhaps the best summation of Alexander's character comes from the acute observations of Prince Metternich (Austrian Foreign Minister 1809–48 and one of the most powerful diplomatic figures in Europe):

1   The Emperor seized an idea, and followed it out quickly. It grew in his mind for about two years, till it came to be regarded by him as a system. In the course of the third year he remained faithful to the system he had adopted and learned to love, listened with real fervour to its promot-
5   ers, and was inaccessible to any calculation as to its worth or dangerous consequences. In the fourth year the sight of these consequences began to calm down his fervour; the fifth year showed an unseemly mixture of the old and nearly extinct system with the new idea. This new idea was often diametrically opposed to the one he had just left.

Yet, despite this judgement, Metternich saw that Alexander's 'disposition was noble, and his word was sacred'.

Alexander's underlying aims did not change during this period. He wanted what was best for his people. What did change, however, were the expectations of many Russians and the Tsar's views of what the best interests of the Russian state really were.

It is not surprising that at the end of the 'War of Liberation' of 1812–15 many Russians believed that the Tsar, who had brought freedom to so much of Europe and expounded so many forward-looking ideas, would come home to bring similar benefits to his own people. Alexander did indeed intend to bring benefits to the

Russian people, but not in the way his more liberal contemporaries hoped. He now saw his 'duty' as extending beyond Russia's frontiers to the rest of Europe. If he was to play a leading role in international affairs, as he was determined to do, he had to ensure that Russia maintained her pre-eminent position amongst the European powers.

a) The Military Colonies

The first major reform Alexander embarked on was the expansion of the system of Military Colonies, which thus far had been limited to one small experiment. The Military Colonies were set up by ordering all the men from a particular regiment to report to a chosen area with their families. When they arrived they would work with the existing peasants to clear away all the old buildings and to create a completely new settlement. This was constructed according to clear, modern and well thought out plans supplied by the Special Corps of Military Colonies.

The soldiers, their families, the existing peasants and the future children of all became subject to strict regimentation in these colonies for life. All members of the colony were subject to the control of specially appointed officers. They were told when to work and at what. They were told whom to marry and when, and even how many children to have. The initial quota was set at one child per year per couple. Married women deemed capable of having children were fined if they did not produce them on schedule. Alexander hoped in one move to improve the situation of a significant number of peasants and their families by giving them access to new land and getting them to use more efficient methods, and to improve the nature and efficiency of Russia's standing army. This laudable aim did partially succeed in its intention, and at first was welcomed by many liberals as a move away from serfdom, but it soon became the focus for the most severe criticisms.

Over a quarter of the standing army became colonists. The colonies, some of which were maintained up to 1857, did bring material benefits. They were far more efficient than traditional estates. Living conditions, especially housing, food, clothing and security, were well above the norm for the period. However, this did not mean that the colonies were liked by those who were in them. Soldiers who had become accustomed to military life did not react well to suddenly finding themselves in full uniform behind an ox-drawn plough. Sporadic revolts took place, which were met with speedy and brutal punishment. The peasants found themselves subject to the same harsh regime. Whole villages begged to be exempted from becoming members of the colonies and losing what they saw as their traditional freedoms. At best they proved reluctant converts to their new way of life.

Vigel, a contemporary critic, summed up the shortcomings of the Military Colonies:

1 Two conflicting vocations were joined in one yoke; the farmer was made to take up the gun and the soldier the plough; the poor colonists were condemned to perpetual forced labour ... Everything was in the Prussian manner, everything was subject to accounting, everything was 5 by weight and measure. Exhausted by labour in the fields, the Military Colonists were formed into ranks and drilled.

The reluctance of the colonists was increased by the very strict discipline they faced. This was largely due to General Arakcheyev's control of the colonies from 1816. Arakcheyev was noted as a strict and brutal disciplinarian in an age when strict discipline was the norm. He became the focal point for liberal grievances. As Alexander increasingly left the day-to-day administration of the Empire to him, Arakcheyev's own particular, ruthlessly efficient, but soulless brand of administration grew steadily more prevalent throughout the Empire. Alexander's attitude to such harsh discipline seems to have been that it was a regrettable necessity. After Arakcheyev had put down one revolt in the Military Colonies, he wrote to Alexander describing how he was torn between his feelings as a Christian and the need to act decisively. He decided on sending the offenders 12 times through a gauntlet of 1,000 men, each man administering one blow to the offender on each run through the gauntlet. This was a common form of punishment, except for the fact that once through the gauntlet was more normal. 25 of the offenders died, not unnaturally as each of them should have received 12,000 blows! Alexander replied, 'I know exactly how your sensitive soul must have suffered in these circumstances'.

b) Education, Golitsyn and Reform

The second major area of reform that Alexander promoted was in the field of education. He felt that the existing educational system was inefficient and lacked the necessary rigour to produce men of the calibre needed by the army and the civil service. Alexander was increasingly preoccupied by his feeling of being a chosen agent of God's will. Therefore, he felt that the person to oversee this reform should be a man of deep religious conviction. He chose Prince Gregory Golitsyn, who had long been his friend and who had been partly responsible for his growing personal interest in religion.

Golitsyn had been Over Procurator of the Holy Synod since 1803. This was a very influential government post, which entailed overseeing the activities of the Orthodox Church. He was also head of the Russian Bible Society, which had recently been formed with the intention of translating the Bible into Russian. Now, in 1817, he became head of the new Ministry of Spiritual Affairs and Education. He believed in the Scriptures as the basis of all truth. With these credentials, one might have expected him to be the arch traditionalist. This he most certainly was not. He was a man of remarkable toleration for the time, despite the fact that he expelled the Jesuits. He naturally had a leaning towards the Orthodox Church, but he also expressed interest in, and a friendly disposition towards, Catholics, Lutherans and even the Quakers. This did not please the Orthodox bishops.

Golitsyn's main aim was for as many people as possible to read the Bible so that they could discover divine truth for themselves. He believed the Scriptures provided the only effective antidote to free-thinking rationalism, which he saw as being a major cause of the problems that faced Russian and indeed European society at the time. This 'freethinking' was at the heart of the 'Enlightenment' of the previous century and involved questioning all existing social and political structures.

The guiding tenet of the new ministry was laid down by Alexander at its inception. He stated that he expected that from then onwards 'Christian piety would be the basis of all true education'. One must presume that, as Alexander chose Golitsyn to head the new ministry, he expected this sentiment to be implemented with a degree of liberality. Yet although Golitsyn did have liberal aims, he was not an able enough administrator to control the hundreds of civil servants – most of whom were far less liberal than himself – who would have to put his beliefs into practice.

Within a short space of time the new ministry earned the nickname of 'Ministry of Darkness'. Those who administered policies tended to take the Tsar's statement at face value, in a narrow and very restrictive way. Even conservative commentators felt that the new ministry went far beyond reasonable bounds. An often-quoted example was the banning by the censors of a book on poisonous mushrooms. They argued that as mushrooms formed the main food of the Orthodox during Lent, they were sacred and that therefore to describe them as being poisonous was sacrilege. Both literature and the theatre also came under increasing scrutiny lest they exert a 'corrupting influence'.

The universities also suffered, Kazan being the clearest example. In 1819, Magnitsky, an officer in the Ministry of Education, was sent to inspect Kazan University. Magnitsky was an extreme example of the bigoted and narrow-minded Russian administrator. He found a hotbed of radical 'freethinking', and recommended to the Tsar that the University be closed down immediately. Alexander was not prepared to go that far, but he made Magnitsky the head of the Kazan educational district, and gave him the task of purging the University of dangerous ideas and influences. He set about the task with fervour, dismissing the director and almost half the academic staff and replacing them with pious but ill-qualified substitutes. He removed hundreds of books which he considered suspect, including those of Newton and Copernicus. He imported Bibles by the case. He ordered that lecture notes be regularly examined, and employed people to listen closely to general student conversations to ensure that they did not contain any impious sentiments. Students who exhibited such tendencies were made to wear signs branding them 'sinner'. Serious offenders were put into solitary confinement, whilst the rest of the student body prayed for their salvation. Kazan was the outstanding case of such repression, but all the universities suffered similar interference to some degree, with the notable exception of Moscow, which escaped – perhaps due to the fact that it was the oldest and most respected of the universities.

c) Liberal Reaction

Young liberals became increasingly frustrated with what they saw as a growing tide of repression. As one Guards officer, who had returned from France, later wrote:

> Seeing the insipid life in St. Petersburg and listening to the babblings of old men praising the past and deprecating every progressive step was unbearable. We were a hundred years from them.

In 1818 a number of these liberals formed a secret society called the 'Union of Welfare' to try to put their views into practice. Their feelings were heightened by the continued liberal stance of Alexander abroad. He encouraged constitutional development in Poland, including the emancipation of serfs in 1816. He supported the granting of constitutions by the German princes and at first appeared to support the nationalist revolt of the Greeks against the Turks. Yet he stood firmly against any such liberal moves at home.

It would be simplistic, however, to argue that Alexander was repressive at home and liberal abroad. The Tsar had not yet become a reactionary. It was just that, by concentrating on affairs abroad, he allowed reactionary elements at home to dominate. Between 1816 and 1820, he spent two-thirds of his time out of the country. He left the running of the Empire largely in the hands of Golitsyn and Arakcheyev. The former was incapable of controlling the reactionary inclinations of his subordinates, whilst the latter, a bureaucrat by nature, believed that opposition needed to be dealt with ruthlessly. The Tsar had not lost his liberal tendencies: he felt, rather, that he had found a higher purpose. What he thought of as a God-given mission to serve the greater good of mankind now occupied him more than domestic considerations.

Even so, Alexander had not completely forgotten Russia. In 1818 Arakcheyev submitted proposals for emancipating Russian serfs. In 1819 Speransky was appointed as Governor of Siberia and was given the task of reforming the administration. In 1818 Alexander asked Novosiltsev to draw up a constitution. Novosiltsev based his draft constitution largely on the Polish model. The Tsar was to remain the sole source of authority in the Empire, but 'the representative assembly of the state' was to assist the sovereign. Regional assemblies were to discuss local affairs and to nominate members of the national assembly. The draft also guaranteed basic civil liberties. Novosiltsev presented it to Alexander early in 1820. Today the draft does not appear particularly liberal. For example, the national assembly was only to meet every five years. Nonetheless, it would have been a major step forward for Russia and might have provided the basis for future constitutional developments. It was certainly considered sufficiently revolutionary 11 years later for Nicholas I to order all printed copies to be burned. There is no reason to suppose that Alexander I might not have attempted to implement the charter had other events not intervened.

d) Repression

The year 1820 seems to mark the real end of Alexander's struggle to remain a liberal autocrat. He believed that events threatened both the international order and the order within his own empire. Successive revolutions in Spain, Naples and Portugal forced the granting of constitutions or brought constitutional monarchs to the throne. The Tsar believed that there was an international conspiracy against Christianity and monarchy, founded on the 'so-called philosophy of Voltaire [a famous French philosopher of the 18th century] and his like'. He urged strong and vigorous action against the revolutionaries. This was very much an about-face for the former pupil of La Harpe. Alexander recognised this quite clearly in a statement to Metternich:

> From 1813 to 1820 is seven years, and these seven years are like a century to me. In 1820 I will at no price do what I did in 1813. You are not altered but I am. You have nothing to regret, but I have.

Alexander was thinking here about international events. However, news brought to him at the Congress of Troppau (see page 107) in November 1820 turned his attention back to domestic affairs. The Semyonovsky Guards, one of the Tsar's own elite and favourite regiments, had mutinied in St Petersburg. Alexander would not have been unduly surprised at the news of a small peasant revolt. Indeed throughout the previous year there had been continuing unrest in the Cossack region. Nor would he have been more than displeased and perhaps disappointed to hear of further unrest in the Military Colonies. But mutiny in one of his own elite regiments was almost beyond his comprehension.

The Semyonovsky revolt itself did not involve violence or bloodshed. The Guards had complained about their treatment and had refused to disperse when ordered to do so. Then they had quietly accepted arrest. But such action still constituted mutiny and was almost without precedent. The subsequent report from St Petersburg laid the blame for the revolt squarely upon the new commander, Colonel Schwarz. He had introduced a degree of rigid discipline which went far beyond normal standards, even in those rigorous times. The report naturally recommended firm punishment, but did not ascribe political motives to the revolt.

Alexander, however, felt that this was another example of the 'international conspiracy'. He could not believe that the men could have mutinied without the encouragement of their officers. He felt that the officers must have wished to distract him from his task of quelling revolution abroad. Arakcheyev's power and influence now grew and repression became the norm. The role of the secret police was expanded and censorship became progressively tighter under their influence. In the end even Golitsyn fell from grace because he offended the censor. This is perhaps not surprising since he authorised the publication of a work, prepared by the Bible Society, which suggested that the Virgin Mary had given birth to sons fathered by Joseph. The Orthodox Church viewed such a suggestion as blasphemy and yet another example of dangerous free-thinking. Censorship became so strict that an anonymous article by Magnitsky, which strongly attacked the whole idea of constitutions, was rejected on the grounds that no comment needed to be made on constitutions. If any comment were needed the government would provide it. In such a climate, Golitsyn had gone too far and the Tsar dismissed him from his post. Shishkov replaced him as Minister of Education. Shishkov was an ageing reactionary, well-known for his view that education was dangerous and subversive in anything more than very small doses. He was therefore an ideally safe candidate for the Ministry of Education.

e) Revolutionary Plans

The Union of Welfare was not inactive during this period of growing repression. In 1821, its leaders examined their position carefully. They feared, rightly, that informers had infiltrated their organisation. They therefore disbanded with the intention of re-forming almost immediately, taking far greater care over whom they admitted to their ranks. The ploy worked. An official report was sent to Alexander stating that the Union, which he had not even heard of up to this point, had existed but had now broken up. The Union developed into two secret organisations, which were geographically based: the Northern Society and the Southern Society. Both grew rapidly. Most new members were young officers. They were inspired by their experience abroad and by the example of the few Spanish officers who had obtained a constitution for their country by leading a revolt there in 1820. They were embittered by what they saw at home. The Southern Society, led by Paul Pestel, was always the better organised and the more active, but the Northern Society also became increasingly to think that direct action might be needed.

By 1825, they had decided that they needed to take drastic action. They would be ready to assassinate Alexander in the summer of 1826. They were convinced that the officers involved in the two societies would easily be able to persuade their men to follow them, and that they would be able to set up a provisional assembly after the assassination. However, their plans lacked firm detail. As yet they had not even agreed on what type of constitutional government they sought. Their plans were so imprecise that they might well have come to nothing had not Alexander precipitated a crisis both by his death and by the fact that he had not made public the arrangements for his succession.

In 1822, Alexander had persuaded the Grand Duke Constantine, his elder brother and next in line of succession, to renounce his claim to the throne. Alexander did this because Constantine had no children to continue the dynasty, and because, since Constantine's remarriage to a non-royal Polish Countess, any future children he might have would not be able to come to the Russian throne legally.

Constantine readily agreed and confirmed his agreement in writing. Alexander then issued a secret decree naming his younger brother Nicholas, who did have a son, as his heir. He told only a few close advisers of this arrangement. Even Nicholas did not know of it! We do not know for sure why he kept this secret. Probably it was because, finding the throne a burden himself, he did not wish the prospect of succession to spoil the relatively carefree life that Nicholas was enjoying.

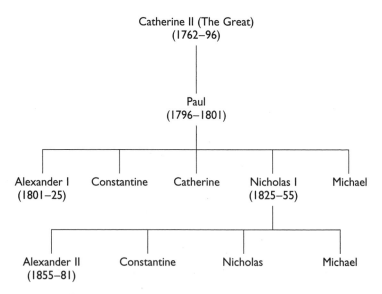

The Romanovs – Catherine the Great to Alexander II

Alexander's last months saw him apparently losing touch with reality. His wife was ill and he seems to have been preoccupied with her health and in making amends to her for his well-known relationship with his mistress. He decided to spend the winter in the southern town of Tagnarog, which was unpopular both because of its climate and its isolation. After he left St Petersburg he received a letter from Arakcheyev, stating that he had had to abandon his duties and retire to his estates in mourning. His notoriously cruel mistress, Nastasya Minkin, had provoked her serfs once too often and had been murdered by them. Shortly afterwards Alexander received a report about the activities of the Southern Society, which contained enough detail to mention Pestel, its leader, by name. Perhaps because he did not have Arakcheyev to consult, the Tsar decided against taking any immediate action. He went on a short tour of the Crimea, where he fell ill. Returning to Tagnarog, he died a fortnight later on 19 November 1825, after a brief illness.

There has been much controversy over Alexander's death. Persistent rumours held that he did not die, but faked his death so that he could slip into obscurity as a wandering mystic. These rumours were encouraged by three main factors: the strange choice of the isolated Tagnarog as a place to spend the winter; the fact he had stated more than once his wish to lay aside the responsibility of office as soon as was practicable; and later by the fact that when his coffin was opened, by Alexander III, it was found to be empty. It is unlikely that these rumours will ever be conclusively proved or disproved. What is certain, however, is that in November 1825, Alexander ceased to be Tsar of Russia. What is also certain is that he contributed to the confusion after his death, by not taking decisive action against the Southern Society and by not clearly settling the matter of his succession. This inaction was a significant factor in bringing about the Decembrist Revolt (see page 33).

4 Assessment

> **KEY ISSUE** What factors best explain the 'liberal' and 'reactionary' phases of Alexander's reign?

In terms of what actually took place, one may divide Alexander's reign in two: a period of apparent liberalism followed by a period of reaction and repression. Yet this interpretation is misleading, first because it gives the impression that Alexander was in full control of what happened, and second because it provides too sharp a division.

There was an almost inevitable dualism present throughout Alexander's reign. After all, he wished to be a *liberal autocrat!* This meant that he had to balance the forces of change against the need to maintain the stability of the autocratic system, of which he was both figurehead and foundation. Even towards the very end of his reign, just before he left for Tagnarog and after the most active period of repression, he expressed the hope that he might be able to grant his people a constitution. This does not fit in with the picture of a reactionary monarch.

It may be that his official biographer, Schilder, writing at the end of the nineteenth century, was correct in describing Alexander as a spent force after 1815:

> The whole store of Alexander's will power seemed spent in his struggle with Napoleon, which placed the utmost strain on all his physical and spiritual strength, and it is not surprising that the Tsar displayed fatigue and mental exhaustion.

This would be a very elegant explanation if it could be sustained. The problem with it is that after 1815 Alexander was remarkably active in the field of foreign affairs, displaying great tenacity and achieving significant success. Perhaps Speransky's judgement that Alexander was 'too weak to rule, too strong to let others rule' contains more truth. But 'too weak' in what sense? He was too weak to implement many of the reforms he wanted, in the way he wanted. The real question is, was he too weak because he lacked the nerve to force through his reforms, or because he was too busy with foreign affairs, or was it that he was unable to overcome the near-immobility of the Russian state? All three factors are important, but when faced by overwhelming conservative pressure, Alexander did give way. In 1812 he dismissed Speransky, and in 1824 he dismissed Golitsyn. It may be that he lost heart somewhat in terms of domestic reform and was naturally enticed towards foreign affairs, where he seemed to be able to attain greater and more rapid success. However, he did not forget the idea of a constitution. In 1818 and in 1825 he expressed a clear desire to implement such a project. The surprising fact is not that he could not find a way of doing so, but rather that he seriously contemplated such a move at all.

It seems that Alexander did sincerely wish to be a 'liberal autocrat'. Whilst it is true that he failed in the eyes of many contemporaries and more recent critics, it is also true that many of his contemporaries saw him as far too liberal. This view was certainly held by many of his fellow monarchs and the conservative elite in Russia itself. Metternich saw him as a dangerous 'son of the Enlightenment' and took much effort to convince him that the spread of secret societies threatened to undermine the existing social and political order.

In some ways Alexander disappointed so many because he promised so much. He tried to be liberal, whilst remaining an autocrat in an autocratic country. Such a course was never likely to be an easy one to follow. The following statement, by the Tsar to the French ambassador La Ferronays in 1821 concerning the Iberian and Italian peninsulas, helps explain his thinking:

1   I love constitutional institutions and think that every decent man should
love them. But can they be introduced indiscriminately for all peoples?
Not all peoples are ready for the same degree for their acceptance. Of
course, freedom and law, which can be enjoyed by an enlightened
5   nation such as yours, does not suit other ignorant peoples of both
peninsulas.

Summary Diagram
Alexander I 1801–25

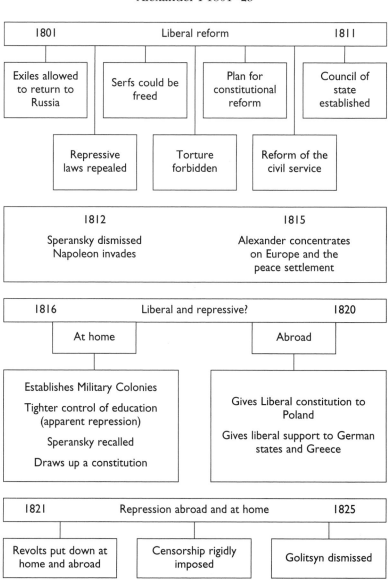

Working on Chapter 2

This chapter concentrates on a ruler who sought to be a liberal auto-crat. Therefore you must be aware of how these contradictions affected his actions. You also need to bring out the ways in which the conservative forces and structures in Russia reacted against reform, and how they often altered the actual impact of reform. The difference between intended outcome and actual outcome is very important. Consider what part the context outlined in Chapter 1 should play in any assessment of Alexander's reign and of Alexander the man.

Answering structured and essay questions on Chapter 2

Consider the following structured question:

a) What was liberal about Alexander's education and his stated intentions at the beginning of his reign? (*4 marks*)
b) What liberal reforms were introduced by Alexander? (*4 marks*)
c) Why did revolutionary movements develop amongst the military during Alexander's reign? (*7 marks*)

Never use 'notes' to answer a structured question. As in an essay, you should use proper sentences. But a structured question is not an essay, and you do not need an introductory paragraph, in which you analyse the question. Instead, you should make relevant points swiftly. You should have little trouble answering the above question, as the relevant factual information is contained in this chapter. Make sure you devote most time and space to part c), which carries the most marks. Perhaps try to divide the reasons into 'general' and 'specific'. Consider also the following essay questions:

1. What were the main aims of Alexander I's domestic policies?
2. How far did Alexander I's liberal education lead to liberal policies and achievements when he became Tsar?
3. 'Enigmatic' - how accurate a description of Alexander I's personality and policies is this?

Question 1 appears to be a straightforward 'what' question. Make a list of the major reforms and initiatives put forward by Alexander. Then put them into a table with the following headings: *Reform or initiative; Motivation; Reaction; Defects.* You should now see the hidden complexity of the question. One underlying aim of Alexander's reforms was to create a strong Russia. Most of his subjects shared that aim. The problem is that there were different views on how to achieve it. Alexander himself was always caught between the desire to reform and improve, and the desire to maintain power and stability. In particular the column marked 'Reaction' should have raised the very important question of reaction from *whom*? Many reforms generated positive and negative reactions. Similarly the motivation behind Golitsyn's reforms was not shared by many who put them into practice. This becomes important when you consider that the majority of Alexander's later domestic policies were not actually his, but were the policies of those he gave power to.

Bearing these issues in mind draw up an essay plan for question 1. Try to put Alexander's reforms into groups. You could try 'type of reform' and 'when the reform took place' to see which is most successful. When you have done this, decide which approach is most effective and why.

Questions 2 and 3 have a different emphasis, though they will make use of much the same information as question 1.

Source-based questions on Chapter 2

1. Alexander's Character and Policies
Read the extracts by Metternich on page 19 and by Alexander on pages 24 and 29. Then answer the following questions.

a) What opinion does Metternich have of Alexander? (*3 marks*)

b) Metternich was a very conservative politician who was responsible for Austrian foreign policy. How does this affect the weight we should place on this piece of evidence? (*5 marks*)

c) In his statement to Metternich, Alexander pointed to the vast importance of the years 1813–20. In what ways did his policies change in this period? (*5 marks*)

d) What light does Alexander's statement to La Ferronays in 1821 shed on his reform policies? (*5 marks*)

e) Using these statements, and your own knowledge, explain why Alexander's liberal objectives failed to be fulfilled. (*12 marks*)

3 Nicholas I 1825–55

POINTS TO CONSIDER

In December 1825 the unexpected death of Alexander I, the previous month, triggered an attempted seizure of power by secret societies influenced by Western European political ideas. The military remained loyal, however, and the new Tsar, Nicholas I, was able to secure his power. Thereafter he saw the need to prevent further revolts. He wanted progress, but not liberal progress: he wanted change which left the essential traditions and nature of Russia intact. He wanted to improve the efficiency and strength of the country and to improve the life of its inhabitants, but not at the expense of the autocracy, which he felt was of central importance in maintaining the Russian state. The conflict between these two aims is a key factor in understanding this period. But when estimating Nicholas's reign you also have to take account of circumstances, external factors and the actions of the Tsar's ministers.

KEY DATES

1825   Death of Alexander I; Decembrist Revolt amidst confusion over the succession.
Accession of Nicholas I, determined to prevent another revolt.

1826–36 Imperial Chancery established: Tsar takes more direct control over affairs.

1830   Polish revolt (after revolution in Paris): Tsar determined to quash revolt and halt spread of revolutionary ideas.

1833   Public auction of serfs prohibited, serf families not to be split up. Uvarov appointed as Minister of education.

1835   New Russian legal code implemented.

1836   Publication of the *Philosophical Letter*, development of Westernisation debate.

1836   Fifth Section established to improve administration of state peasants.

1847   Serfs given technical right to buy freedom.

1848   Revolutionary activity across Europe: Tsar determined to control subversive ideas.

1849   Petrashevsky Circle accused of revolutionary activity; no real evidence found but 21 sentenced to death: last-minute reprieve.
150,000 troops crush revolt by Kossuth in Hungary.
Strict control of Universities, student numbers fall.

1853   Crimean War begins; weakness of Russian Empire exposed.

1855   Death of Nicholas I.

1 The Decembrist Revolt

> **KEY ISSUES** What was the Decembrist Revolt? What does it tell us about Russia in 1825 and about Nicholas I?

Three main factors prompted the Decembrist Revolt. The authorities had failed, at the end of Alexander I's reign, to take decisive action against the secret societies. Then confusion over the succession provided the opportunity for the societies to gain support from otherwise loyal elements in Russian society. Thirdly, the justified fear of those societies that their plans had been discovered led to the date for their planned revolt being brought forward.

a) The Succession

When news of Alexander's death arrived in St Petersburg, his secret manifesto (see page 26) was opened and Nicholas was told for the first time that he was to be Tsar. His elder brother, Constantine, had married a Polish catholic and secretly renounced his claim to the throne. Evidence suggests that Nicholas's first thought was to publish the manifesto and proclaim himself Tsar. But Miloradovich, the Governor General of St Petersburg, suggested a more cautious approach. He reminded Nicholas that, according to custom, Constantine should become Tsar immediately on Alexander's death. This, coupled with the fact that Nicholas was far from popular with the Guards, led the governor to suggest that he proclaim Constantine as Tsar, and then wait for Constantine to renounce the throne before proclaiming himself Tsar. Nicholas decided to follow this advice because he was not sure of the Guards' support. He knew that the Guards had intervened in the succession on a number of previous occasions. He therefore proclaimed Constantine as Tsar and sent a courier to Warsaw to tell his brother what he had done.

The situation was complicated by the nature of communications in Russia. News of Alexander's death had reached Constantine in Warsaw two days before it reached Nicholas in St Petersburg. Constantine had proclaimed Nicholas as Tsar, and had written to Nicholas informing him of his action. Hence each brother had proclaimed the other as Tsar. But it took seven days for a message to travel from Warsaw to St Petersburg, and the letters from the two brothers had therefore crossed. On receiving the first letter from Warsaw, Nicholas at once wrote asking Constantine asking to return to the capital. This letter arrived in Warsaw on 2 December. Constantine sent back a peremptory reply stating that he could see no reason for coming to St Petersburg and that he would be grateful if Nicholas would stop bothering him and get on with his duties as Tsar! Several equally fruitless communications followed, which did not alter Constantine's decision.

b) Inaction over the Planned Revolt

This ludicrous situation gave the secret societies a breathing space. They had intended to seize power the following summer. It was now clear that they would have to bring their plans forward, especially as they rightly suspected that part of their plans had been made known to the authorities. The Southern Society was by far the better organised, but the Northern Society was centrally placed in the capital, St Petersburg. However, both groups were determined to act. Intense activity followed, but it involved much more rhetoric than detailed planning. The officers involved seemed to have a blind faith that their troops would follow them, and that the great majority of those who would not actively support them would at least not take direct action against them.

On Saturday 12 December, Nicholas received yet another letter from Constantine. He refused to come to the capital, but confirmed Nicholas as Tsar. Nicholas finally accepted that Constantine would not come, and therefore made plans to publish the manifesto and to proclaim himself Tsar on Monday 14 December. On the same day, Nicholas also received reports giving specific details of the Southern Society and general details of the Northern Society. He was then informed of the plans of the Northern Society by a Lieutenant Rostovstev. There seems little doubt that had Arakcheyev been in place he would have taken decisive action. Governor General Miloradovich, however, was complacent. He assured Nicholas that the situation was under control: the Northern Society's activities were being monitored (which was accurate) and they posed no real threat (which was quite inaccurate). Nicholas decided to accept this reassurance, though he was apparently far from convinced. He did so on the grounds that he feared direct action against the conspirators might both provoke the revolt he sought to avoid and persuade the Guards to support them.

Meanwhile, an extraordinary event occurred which gives an insight into the peculiar nature of Russian society at the time. Rostovstev, who had given the Tsar details of the Northern Society's activities, went from the Tsar to inform the Northern Society of his meeting with him. By his own lights, he was acting honourably. He had fulfilled his duty by keeping the Tsar informed of events; and now he preserved his own conscience by informing the Society's members of his action. It seems that his aim was to prevent the revolt, without harming his comrades. But Rostovstev's news naturally caused panic within the Society. The officers involved had planned to accuse Nicholas of seizing the throne from the legitimate ruler Constantine and thus convince their troops of the just nature of their cause. Some officers quietly withdrew from the scheme at this point, but others decided to continue with their plans.

c) The Day of the Revolt

On the morning of Monday 14 December, while the great majority of Guards calmly took their oath of allegiance to the new Tsar, the rebels gathered in the Senate Square of St Petersburg to demand that Constantine be maintained as Tsar. Miloradovich was still convinced that the matter could be settled without resorting to force. He went alone to talk to the rebels and to explain their error to them. As he was about to leave, having failed to convince them to go back to their barracks, he was shot by one of the more radical members of the group. He died later that day.

Nicholas then decided to take charge of the situation himself. The rebels had believed that certainly 8,000, and possibly up to 20,000, troops would join them. In fact, their numbers never rose above 3,000. They were surrounded by some 10,000 loyal troops. Nicholas decided that a show of force would convince the rebels to retire. He ordered the cavalry to charge. What followed might have been funny, if the situation had not been so serious. The horses could not maintain a footing on the icy cobbles, and their charge was broken up by one volley from the rebels. For the next three hours the two forces faced each other, whilst Nicholas made repeated attempts to persuade the rebels to return to their barracks. He wanted to avoid bloodshed, which might arouse others and make the situation more dangerous. As for the rebels, they simply did not know what to do, except to wait and hope that others would rally to their banner. A few did so, but not enough to make any difference to the situation. As the light began to fail, after the rebels had been in the square for over five hours, Nicholas was finally persuaded to take firm action. He ordered the artillery to open fire. Within minutes the 'Decembrist Revolt' was at an end.

Nicholas described events as follows:

1 I saw the regiment of Grenadier Guards, in complete disorder, walking in a body with their colours but without officers. Suspecting nothing, I approached them, wanting to stop the men and place them in formation, but when I called out 'Halt!' they replied: 'We're for Constantine!'

5 I indicated them Senate Square and said: 'In that case, that's your way.' And the entire throng walked past me, through all the troops, and joined without hindrance their equally misguided comrades. This was fortunate, for otherwise bloodshed would have begun under the windows of the palace, and our fate would have been more than doubtful.

10 Then Adjutant General Vasil'chikov turned to me and said: 'Sire, there is not a moment to lose; there is nothing else to do now. We must use grapeshot!' I had foreseen the necessity of this, but, I confess, when the time came, I could not make up my mind to such a measure. I was terror-stricken. 'Do you wish me to spill the blood of my subjects on the first day of my reign?' I

15 replied to Vasil'chikov. 'In order to save your reign,' he answered me.

These words brought me back to myself; coming to my senses, I saw that I must either take it upon myself to spill the blood of a few and almost surely save everything, or spare myself at the cost of definitely sacrificing the state ...

20 At that point, seeing no other alternative, I ordered: 'Fire!'

The revolt in the north was over. The much better organised revolt in the region was, thanks to firm action by the authorities, also soon dealt with. However, this traumatic beginning to his reign could not but affect the new Tsar.

d) Assessment

Historians have characterised the Decembrist Revolt in two different ways: as a traditional Russian aristocratic *coup*, and as a forerunner of the popular movements that sought to remove the Tsarist autocracy. There are elements of truth in both views.

The Decembrists included members of the country's most aristocratic families. Their revolt was a traditional *coup* in that the great majority of the Decembrists did not even contemplate involving the mass of the people. They intended to rely on winning over substantial elements of the army. But it was more than a traditional palace *coup*, like those which had brought Catherine II and Alexander I to the throne. The Decembrists did wish to change the system, even if they could not agree in what way. Many of the officers involved had been inspired by what they had seen in France at the end of the Napoleonic wars. There was a general agreement that change was necessary. Muraviev, the leader of the Northern Society, wanted a federal system based on the American model, with the Tsar effectively filling the position of President. Pestel, the leader of the Southern Society, accepted regicide as a necessary evil and sought to establish a republican system where 'all Russian citizens should exercise equally all individual rights, civil and political', even if those rights were to be limited by a strong central government. Although not all the conspirators fully shared the views of either Pestel or Muraviev, these elements do make the Decembrist Revolt something more than just another aristocratic *coup*. It may have appeared traditional in form, but the intent was real change. It was also very public. In that sense at least it can be seen as a move towards the revolutionary movements that were to emerge in the 1870s.

2 The Military Tsar

> **KEY ISSUE** Was Nicholas reactionary and unimaginative, or is such a judgement too simple?

Nicholas's reign began during the turmoil of the Decembrist Revolt, and ended in the disaster of the Crimean War. Critics have argued that his period as Tsar was characterised by repression and an absurd preoccupation with trivial detail. His supporters have pointed to a flowering in the arts, to real progress in the realms of economic and technical endeavour and to a determined attempt to improve the legal and bureaucratic systems. Nicholas's intentions were certainly not matched by results, but in this he was far from alone among nineteenth-century Tsars.

Nicholas had not been brought up, and had no wish, to be Tsar. He had wanted nothing more than to be an efficient, dedicated and effective officer. He had a military respect for order, planning, uniformity and clearly defined lines of responsibility. Yet he dedicated himself wholeheartedly to his duties as Tsar. Unlike Alexander he insisted on being in complete control of events within the Empire. He believed in firm, prompt action and strict discipline. Above all, he believed in the concept of duty to the fatherland, from the highest to the lowest. He applied strict standards to his own conduct and expected no less from his subordinates.

One of the most perceptive analyses of Nicholas comes from Queen Victoria:

1   He is stern and severe – with fixed principles of duty which nothing on
    earth will make him change; very clever I do not think him, and his mind
    is an uncivilised one; his education has been neglected; politics and mili-
    tary concerns are the only things he takes great interest in; the arts and
5   all softer occupations he is insensible to, but he is sincere, I am certain,
    sincere even in his most despotic acts, from a sense that it is the only
    way to govern; he is not, I am sure, aware of the dreadful cases of indi-
    vidual misery which he so often causes, for I can see by various
    instances that he is kept in utter ignorance of many things, which his
10 people carry out in most corrupt ways, while he thinks he is extremely
    just.

a) The Treatment of the Decembrists

Nicholas's first priority was to investigate the nature and causes of the Decembrist Revolt. He was naturally alarmed by the revolt itself, but he was equally disturbed by the fact that the leaders of the revolt were for the most part representatives of Russia's oldest and most respected noble families. This investigation was to become the model for the future. It was extremely thorough and painstaking. Nicholas appointed a special committee, which reported directly to him and in whose proceedings he frequently took an active part. He was determined that the leaders should be firmly punished as an example to all that disloyalty would not be tolerated, no matter what a person's position in society.

In all over 3,000 people were arrested. The majority of the rank and file soldiers were either severely reprimanded or subjected to the standard form of corporal punishment – running the gauntlet (see page 21). Five of the leaders were sentenced to death and 116 were sentenced to exile in Siberia. This may not seem excessively harsh, but in Russia many contemporaries did think it so. This was partly because, technically, the death penalty was illegal. It had not been used since the Pugachev Rebellion, the great peasant revolt of 1775. There was also a long tradition of pardoning those who were exiled, for whatever reason, after a salutary period of isolation away from 'civilised' Russia. In the case of the Decembrists, the exiles were not allowed to return. In Nicholas's defence it should be noted that he commuted the sentence of the five from the barbarous 'quartering' (disembowelment) to hanging, and the sentence of 24 others from execution to exile. However, this did nothing to lessen the feeling that the sentences were unduly harsh.

b) The Tsar's Intentions

Nicholas was not only concerned with making an example of the leaders of the revolt, he also wished to deal with its causes. He wished to do so both in order to prevent a similar occurrence in the future and to remedy the abuse and mismanagement, which the committee had found to be so prevalent in Russian society. However, he did not accept that there was any fault in the idea of autocracy itself. The problems which were clearly detailed by the committee included: corruption and inefficiency in the administration; an antiquated legal system, which had virtually broken down; a deterioration in the economic position of the nobility; and an increasing burden, in terms of both taxation and the need to increase productivity, on the peasant population. The committee produced a comprehensive report on the problems and grievances listed by the accused. Nicholas kept a personal copy of the report and was determined to deal with many of the problems which it listed. He was also determined to limit the 'pernicious' spread of foreign ideas, which he felt must be responsible for the 'misguided' actions of the Decembrists.

Nicholas I made a firm start to the task which he had set himself. The revolt and the report had left him with a mistrust of both the administration and the Russian nobility. He decided that therefore he must keep personal control over the formation and implementation of future policy. This led him to form his own administration, the Imperial Chancery. He also surrounded himself with non-Russian advisers, in particular Benckendorf, Kankrin, Kiselev and Nesselrode. The Chancery had originally been organised to deal with matters that needed the Tsar's personal attention. Nicholas now felt that all aspects of the running of the Empire needed his personal consideration and the Chancery was expanded accordingly. This was not simply a move to take personal control. It was an attempt to bypass the inept bureaucracy of the established administration.

The original Chancery became the First Section of His Majesty's Own Chancery, and it functioned as his private secretariat. In 1826 he established the Second Section to deal with the codification of the Russian legal system. In the same year he established the Third

Section, whose function was to monitor and regulate the activities of all 'suspicious and harmful people'. In 1828, the Fourth Section was set up to monitor and control educational and charitable organisations, which had previously been controlled by the Empress Dowager. Finally, in 1836, a Fifth Section was formed to reorganise the administration of state peasants. This personal administration frequently bypassed normal channels. It gave Nicholas the ability to implement changes quickly, but led to a ridiculous situation in which some ministers did not know of major changes in their own areas, until they were actually decreed by the Tsar. It also led to the Tsar becoming increasingly overloaded with work.

Though Nicholas's treatment of the Decembrists was thought of as unduly severe by many people, some liberals did see reason for optimism. Nicholas's early dismissal of Arakcheyev and Magnitsky, the two members of Alexander's administration most closely associated with reaction, appeared to bode well for the future. This feeling was reinforced by the appointment of Speransky to oversee the codification of the legal system by the Second Section. Nesselrode was maintained as Minister of Foreign Affairs, and Kankrin as Minister of Finance, but neither of these ministries was closely associated with the darker side of Alexander's reign. Nicholas stated clearly in his manifesto that change was needed, but he stated equally clearly his view on who should guide that change:

> It is not by means of insolent and impractical projects, which are destructive, but it is from above, that national institutions are gradually improved, defects remedied, and abuses reformed.

3 The Chancery, Planning and Progress

> **KEY ISSUE** Were the social and economic reforms fostered under Nicholas I a reasonable and coherent response to Russia's problems?

Under Speransky, the Second Section of the Chancery set about its massive task with great speed and vigour. The Russian legal system was in chaos. The most recent code had been produced in 1649. Since then hundreds of laws had fallen into disuse, and hundreds of contradictory laws had been passed. Successive Russian Tsars had tried to deal with this problem, but all had failed to overcome the complexities involved. By 1830, Speransky and his section had compiled a mammoth 45 volumes. The first 40 volumes contained over 30,000 laws, the last five a detailed index and annexes. Speransky then set about producing a code, which contained only active laws, collected and listed by subject.

Speransky had wanted to produce a detailed commentary to accompany the code, but Nicholas vetoed this on the grounds that the laws should speak for themselves. However, Speransky did borrow concepts from foreign legal systems to make the code more coherent. Thus in some ways he circumvented the Tsar's prohibition on a commentary. This code was made up of 15 volumes and was completed at the beginning of 1833. It was put into effect in 1835. From that point onwards the code was regularly revised and updated. The Russian legal system at last had a firm, clear basis from which to work. Its application in practice fell short of Speransky's hopes, but it did provide the foundation necessary for the establishment of a uniform legal system throughout Russia.

a) The Third Section

The Third Section controlled the political, or secret, police. It was headed by General Benckendorf, who had been commander of the Guards under Alexander. On the grounds that the police were inefficient and attracted a very poor calibre of recruit, he suggested the formation of a ministry of police and the overhaul of the whole system. Nicholas, who had a deep distrust of ministries but who sympathised with the aims expressed, refused to set up a new ministry. Instead, he created the Corps of Gendarmes, to be administered by the Third Section under Benckendorf's command.

Benckendorf was determined that the new police should be of the highest possible calibre, and be respected and admired by the populace. Great efforts were made to give this new body a positive image and to separate them in everyone's mind from the ordinary police. The Gendarmes were given bright sky-blue uniforms with white gloves to emphasise their purity of purpose. Within three years Benckendorf reported to the Tsar that 'The Gendarmerie has become moral physician to the people. To it each comes with his ailments and despair.' Though reality fell somewhat short of this grand claim, the 'blue archangels' did win much support in their early years. They received complaints, they rooted out corrupt officials, they prepared cases against unjust landlords, and they even privately advocated progressive changes in the position of serfs. In their early years, therefore, the Gendarmes won much of the respect that Benckendorf sought for them and many of their top officials were welcomed in liberal circles. As time went on, however, they concentrated more on their role as censors and as the suppressors of subversive ideas than on their roles as champions of justice and the enemies of corruption. They also exercised an increasingly repressive influence on education, especially after Uvarov's resignation (see page 49). They became increasingly associated with the reactionary elements of Russian society.

b) The State Peasants

The Fifth Section was created in 1836 to improve the poor administration of the state peasants. The aim was to make them more efficient producers, both for the benefit of the state as a whole and as an example for landowners to follow with their serfs. Kiselev, another German who had been in Russian service since before 1812, was placed at the head of the new section. The following year, Nicholas overcame his dislike of ministries and created the Ministry of State Domains, with Kiselev at its head. He did so specifically to give weight to the project and to show the importance he attached to it.

Kiselev headed the Ministry for the next 18 years and did make considerable progress. New land was surveyed and opened up to landless peasants. Loans were made readily available to the peasants to make improvements on their lands. New crops, particularly the potato, and improved breeding techniques were encouraged and supported. Hospitals, schools and churches were built to cater for over 200,000 peasants who were resettled on new land during this period. Kiselev has been much criticised because the main objective, to turn the state peasants into an efficient and productive group, did not succeed, and because of the authoritarian nature of his reforms. Resettlement was not voluntary. Many peasants naturally resented being forcibly moved and told what they could and could not grow. Kiselev's officials made little attempt to win the support of the peasants. Hence there were periodic riots, particularly between 1841 and 1843, when the introduction of the potato was being forced on the peasants.

These drawbacks must be balanced against the likely condition of the peasantry had these attempts at improvement not been made. Conditions would certainly not have been better. Kiselev attempted to bring about a planned improvement in their conditions. Had the positive effects of these reforms been able to keep pace with the negative effects of rapid population growth, both Nicholas and Kiselev might have been forgiven for the heavy-handed nature of their implementation. As it was, population growth largely outstripped the positive benefits of reform, which therefore led to criticism and unrest rather than appreciation and stability.

c) The Economy

Nicholas also sought to make broader economic progress. Economic policy during this period was largely formulated by Kankrin, another German, who had been in Russian service since 1797 and had distinguished himself in 1812 as quartermaster-general. He was Minister of Finance from 1823 to 1844. Kankrin was a conservative who believed strongly in protecting domestic industries from foreign competition and in balancing the budget. He was determined to reduce the national debt and to stabilise the value of the rouble.

Kankrin was both reactionary and progressive. He opposed the development of a railway system, which he thought would be of little advantage economically, merely serving to encourage travel and the spread of unhealthy ideas. Indeed it is quite possible that no railway development would have taken place in this period but for Nicholas's personal intervention. Yet in other areas Kankrin was progressive. He set up various bodies to consult with Russian manufacturing and business interests, both to explain his plans and to take note of their comments. He fostered an expansion of technical and commercial education, and his ministry encouraged and funded study abroad. He also reorganised the study of both mining and forestry.

Part of Kankrin's poor reputation stems from the fact that it was during this period that Russia fell so far behind Western Europe, particularly England, in terms of production. Yet this was in many ways a product of the social system that existed in Russia. Considerable progress was made in all areas. Foreign trade increased by approximately 250 per cent during Nicholas's reign. What was static was Russia's share of world trade, which remained stable at about 3.7 per cent of the total. Russia increased production and trade at the same rate as the average increase for the rest of the world. What she did not do was to keep pace with the industrial revolution taking place in Western Europe. But this would almost certainly not have been possible without a major transformation in the nature and structure of Russian society.

Kankrin is also rarely given credit for his efforts to stabilise the currency and to reduce inflation, though he did make significant progress in this area. By 1843 he had reduced the number of roubles in circulation to one quarter of their peak level. He had backed the currency firmly by establishing gold and silver reserves, thus stabilising its value at home and abroad, and he had significantly reduced the national debt. He had therefore established some degree of confidence and stability in the monetary system, which should have aided further growth and expansion.

Kankrin retired in 1844 and died the next year. His successors could not match his efforts. Their inefficiency, coupled with the disastrous effects of the Crimean War, left the currency in an even worse situation than it had been in before his reforms. Whilst it is almost certainly true, as his critics assert, that his tight fiscal control did little to free money for investment in industry, he did at least arrest the growing instability of the rouble. Whilst economists will continue to debate the nature of economic growth, a stable currency is generally held to be an important prerequisite for such growth. This Kankrin did achieve during his own period in office, even if his successors could not maintain that stability.

4 The Reactionary Tsar?

KEY ISSUE How did Nicholas I acquire the reputation of being a reactionary?

Inside Russia, Nicholas expanded the rigid centralised control of government, and insisted on conducting much of the activity of his administration in secret. He did this because his reign coincided with the rise of the intelligentsia, who were by nature critical of his rule, and because he was worried about the spread of revolutionary movements from Europe. His own philosophical ideas were summed up by notions of 'Orthodoxy, Autocracy, Nationality'.

a) The Polish Revolt

The Polish revolt of 1830–1 has often been seen as a major turning point in Nicholas's reign. 1830 saw a wave of revolutionary activity in Europe. The July Revolution in Paris, which brought Louis-Philippe to the throne, was followed by the Belgian uprising in September against the Dutch, and unrest in Italy and Germany. This activity naturally worried Nicholas, who feared that its spread would threaten his own throne. He tried to co-ordinate international action against the revolutionaries but received very little support from other governments. He contemplated direct military action to stabilise affairs, but, in late November 1830, he found that revolutionary ideas had spread to his own empire, just as he had feared. The Poles rose in revolt against their Russian overlords. Constantine failed to control the situation and the Polish standing army supported the revolt. It took nine months to suppress the uprising and it cost many lives, including that of Constantine, who died of cholera.

Nicholas was determined to control the Poles. He therefore revoked the constitution and replaced it with a much more restrictive statute. Poland lost its right to a national assembly and a separate army. The Universities of Warsaw and Vilna were closed. In theory Poland retained a separate administration, but in reality, from 1833 until after Nicholas's death, she was ruled under martial law and her administration was placed under increasingly tight Russian control. A deliberate and determined policy of 'russification' (the imposition of Russian ways, institutions and beliefs, and the eradication of local customs, institutions and beliefs) had begun.

b) 'Orthodoxy, Autocracy and Nationality'

There is little doubt that the events of 1830–31 surprised and worried Nicholas. The appointment of Uvarov as Minister of Education in 1833 and the adoption of the doctrine of 'Official Nationality' have been seen as evidence that the Tsar decided on a policy of increased internal repression. Yet Uvarov, though certainly a conservative, was if anything more liberal than his immediate predecessors and did at least have a genuine interest and respect for education. Equally, there was nothing in the doctrine of 'Official Nationality' to suggest a move away from the ideas Nicholas had been expounding since the beginning of his reign. It was adopted because it fitted so closely to his own ideas. Uvarov succinctly summed up 'Official Nationality' as 'Orthodoxy,

Autocracy, Nationality'. These three elements were meant to provide the basis and justification for maintaining Russia against harmful influences for change, especially of a revolutionary or democratic nature.

'Orthodoxy' was taken to have two main elements. The first emphasised the relationship between Tsar, God and the Orthodox Church, with the Tsar as the rightful, undisputed ruler placed on his throne 'by God's special grace'. The second element centred on the precepts of the Church as a guide to human action. Piety was taken as the main yardstick in human behaviour and life in 'this world' was not held to be nearly as important as that in the 'next world'.

'Autocracy' represented the traditional Russian view of the total submission to the Tsar of all his subjects. The 'Little Father' was fully responsible for his people's spiritual and physical welfare: he and only he could really see what was best for them. He might need to be harsh on occasion; but what he did, he did for the benefit of all. He had to protect them from themselves in case they allowed themselves to be infected by foreign ideas such as freedom and democracy. He had to keep Russia strong and powerful lest the Empire succumb to foreign threats to the harm of his 'children'.

'Nationality' meant essentially the promotion of Russian culture and institutions as something to be treasured and preserved, the fostering of a patriotic spirit and the distinct identity of Russia separate from the rest of Europe. This spirit was taken by the more extreme supporters of nationality as the justification for demanding the 'russification' of all the lands and people on the edges of the Empire. Whilst Nicholas may have been pleased at the patriotic nature of these demands, the fact that he resisted them is important. Above all, Nicholas desired a calm and well-ordered society. He would not introduce change unless it was necessary and certain to bring clear benefits. Thus Finland and the Baltic states were left virtually untouched, because they were considered loyal. Where there was revolt or open opposition, however, as in Poland and Transcaucasia, local institutions were largely swept away to be replaced by Russian institutions and governors.

c) The Secret Committees

This desire to ensure that change was introduced only when clearly necessary runs deep throughout Nicholas's reign. It was coupled with a strong desire to prevent the general population from coming into contact with new ideas for fear of what this might lead to. This desire led to a proliferation of secret committees, which were established throughout his reign.

The first such committee was established in December 1826. Its task was to consider the state papers left by Alexander, and the condition of Russia in general, and to make suggestions as to what should be altered to improve the situation which the Decembrist report had highlighted (see page 38). The committee was so secret that Kankrin, who was called before it to give advice on financial considerations, was not even informed of its nature and purpose. The committee laboured for six painstaking years. It only produced very minor suggestions for modifying the existing system, yet even these recommendations were not put into practice.

Nicholas subsequently set up further secret committees with more clearly defined tasks. The very secrecy of these committees made it appear that Nicholas was more reactionary than he actually was. It appeared that he was doing nothing and considering no change. In fact he was almost constantly considering change, though always from the top and under his personal control.

d) The Serfs

Nine committees were set up to examine the question of serfdom. These committees were also kept secret in case rumours of emancipation led to unrest. Nicholas did enact several measures to improve the situation of the serfs. In 1827 he set out clear limitations to landowners' rights to send serfs to Siberia. In 1833 he prohibited the selling of serfs by public auction, the splitting up of serf families and the 'mortgaging' of serfs without land to obtain credit. In 1842 it was made technically easier for serfs to buy their freedom. Finally, in 1847, serfs were given the right to buy their freedom if their village was sold at public auction.

This might appear to be an impressive list, but in practice it made little or no difference to the great majority of serfs. They were largely unable to take advantage of their new 'rights'. Nicholas knew that real change had to come, since he believed that serfdom failed on both economic and moral grounds. But he was prevented from taking more effective action, in part by the concerted opposition he faced. Two other factors were arguably of greater significance in limiting the measures he took and were always in the forefront of his mind: the need to prevent the unrest that new ideas might generate, and the perceived need to bolster the landowning nobility. The nobility were decreasing steadily in number and power as they sank into increasing debt. Nicholas's feelings are summarised in this passage from his speech to the State Council in 1842:

> 1 There is no question that serfdom in its present state in our country is
> an evil, palpable and obvious to everyone. However, to attack it *now*
> would be, of course, an even more disastrous evil ... The Pugachev
> rebellion [a two-year peasant revolt in the 1770s] showed how far mob
> 5 violence can go. Fortunately, later occurrences of this sort have always,
> until now, been suppressed ... But we must not conceal from ourselves
> the fact that current ideas are not the same as those that existed pre-
> viously, and it is clear to every reasonable observer that the present
> situation cannot last forever.

This fear of instituting real change severely limited the possibilities open to Nicholas. Whilst maintaining an overall system as inherently rigid as an autocracy, there is limited scope for improving the basic features of that system.

e) Education and Censorship

The most stringent criticism of Nicholas's reign is usually reserved for the fields of education and censorship. Uvarov was Minister of Education from 1833 to 1849. Along with the Third Section, he was also in charge of censorship. Uvarov was an intellectual, with a great love of the classics, who had resigned his post as head of the St Petersburg educational region in 1819 in protest at repressive actions taken against the University. But though Uvarov might have been liberal in comparison with his predecessors, he was conservative even by Russian standards. He was a staunch defender of serfdom and believed firmly that education should be tailored to the status of the people receiving it. He sought firm control over education throughout Russia. Private schools and private tutors were made directly responsible to the state for what they taught. A large inspectorate was built up to ensure that teaching conformed to the rules laid down by his ministry. Above all, he wished to prevent the spread of 'improper ideas'. He wanted to instill in the young a respect for Russian institutions and a love of their country. At first many people felt that Uvarov was making positive moves, and he did actively encourage developments in the 'safe' areas of scientific and technical research. Yet, as he steadily increased the centralised nature of his control over the education system, and as the list of restrictions grew, the number and volume of his critics steadily increased.

It was censorship that aroused the most opposition. Responsibility for censorship was shared between the Ministry of Education and the Third Section. It was often as arbitrary as it had been at the end of Alexander's reign. A cookery book was not allowed to mention 'free air' because it sounded too revolutionary, and any discussion of social issues was frowned upon. Although censorship raised a great deal of opposition, it did not become as all-encompassing as it had been in the final years of Alexander until the end of Nicholas's reign. This is perhaps best illustrated by the following extract from an anonymous article, which was passed by the censor in 1836. It was published in the Moscow periodical *The Telescope* as a 'Philosophical Letter' from 'Necropolis' (The City of the Dead).

1   We have never progressed in keeping with other peoples of the world [but] exist as if in banishment outside the times, untouched by the universal education of mankind ... [In Europe] each person is fully possessed of his rights and easily gathers the ideas that have spread
5   throughout society and uses them for his advantage ... They are the concepts of duty, justice, law, and order...
      Despite the fact that we are called Christians, we did not move when Christianity, leaving the past behind it, progressed along the path

solemnly indicated by the Divine Founder. While the world entirely
10 rebuilt itself, we built nothing but continued in our mud huts...
   Though our limited mental habits, traditions, and memories do not
link us to any peoples of the world ... we still belong to the Western
world. This link still makes our destiny dependent on European society.
Therefore the more we try to affiliate ourselves with it, the better off
15 we shall be...

One contemporary saw the letter as a 'merciless cry of reproach and
bitterness against Russia'. It was a cry that was to be echoed by a growing group of 'Westernisers' and liberals.

Nicholas reacted in a characteristically thorough and resolute
manner. The censor who had passed the article was dismissed, *The
Telescope* was closed down and its publisher was sent into exile. The
author of the letter, Chadaev, was discovered, declared insane and
confined to house arrest, though he was well treated in his captivity.
In a few months, after renouncing the more extreme of his views, he
was allowed back into circulation and was once more prominent at
intellectual gatherings.

Perhaps because periodicals were generally more careful about
how far they went, only three were actually closed down during the
whole of Nicholas's reign. Censorship did not actually disrupt the
intellectual pursuits of the intelligentsia very much. If anything, it
acted as a spur to them. What censorship did do was prevent the free
spread of ideas outside the narrow confines of this group. It was also
very severe in individual cases, especially in the case of the daily press,
which suffered more than the journals. It was therefore effective in
promoting the view of the Tsar and his administration as narrow and
repressive in outlook, rather than, as was intended, actually in stifling
debate.

f) Westernisers and Slavophiles

The 'Philosophical Letter' pointed to the growth of two increasingly
important and influential groups in Russian society: the
'Westernisers' and the 'Slavophiles'.

* The Westernisers, mostly liberal in outlook, held that Russia had
  much to learn from Western Europe about social organisation
  and government. They pointed to Peter the Great as a Tsar who
  had moved Russia in a modern and progressive direction to the
  benefit of all.
* The Slavophiles were closer to Nicholas's ideas on Orthodoxy
  and Autocracy. They believed in the inherent superiority of
  Orthodoxy as a moral force and saw the Tsar, an autocratic Tsar,
  as the unifying symbol of the Russian state. They embodied a type
  of romantic spiritualism, which saw in the peasant commune an
  idealised form of society based on fraternal love, freedom and

spiritual purity. They believed that the commune had developed from Slavic traditions under the guiding hand of the Orthodox Church. They also felt that further development of the commune would enable Russia to avoid unhealthy western influences, which to them rested on an unholy, and much too worldly, basis of individualism, rationalism and competition. Slavophiles wanted progress, but firmly within Russian traditions as they saw them. To them, Peter the Great was a dangerous aberration.

The Westernisers' view is perhaps best summarised by Belinsky in his *Letter to Gogol*, in which he criticised the author, whose previous works he had respected and supported, for praising existing Russian society:

1   You failed to realise that Russia sees her salvation, not in mysticism, nor in asceticism, nor pietism, but in the successes of civilisation, enlightenment, and humanity ... I leave it to your conscience to admire the divine beauty of autocracy (it is both safe and profitable), but continue to
5   admire it judiciously from your beautiful faraway; at close quarters it is not so attractive and not so safe.

The letter was not officially published for over 50 years, but it became widely discussed inside Russia and came to the attention of the Third Section. The grapevine of the intelligentsia was efficient and effective at carrying the news that it wished to carry. Ideas were also spread under a number of guises in various journals. Belinsky, for example, had successfully put forward his ideas over the previous eight years as the chief literary critic of a St Petersburg journal.

    Censorship was annoying. It was arbitrary and unfair. It was a focal point for opposition. It certainly did not encourage free and open debate, but it was not until after 1848, as in other areas of Russian life, that it really began to bite.

5 The Last Seven Years

> **KEY ISSUE** Was this period very different from the rest of Nicholas's reign?

The latter part of Nicholas's reign was a stern period of repression. The rebellions, which swept across Europe during 1848, worried leaders of all political complexions. Nicholas, being the most autocratic, had perhaps most reason to be concerned. This concern was increased by the fact that Russia's two main conservative allies, Prussia and Austria, were now ruled by ageing and increasingly indecisive leaders. This had prompted Nicholas to say: 'Once we were three, but now we are one and a half. I don't count Prussia, and Austria counts for only a half.' The first results of the revolutions confirmed his worst fears. Frederick William of Prussia compromised with the rebels, and in Austria Metternich was relieved of office and universal male suffrage accepted. As the tide of revolt spread, Nicholas even asked Queen Victoria to stand with him against these dangerous and unholy movements. Predictably, Victoria declined the invitation.

Internal events served to increase Nicholas's fears. There was a severe cholera epidemic and the worst crop failure in 30 years, which led to the price of bread more than doubling. Nicholas once more took firm and decisive action. 400,000 troops were moved to the western borders to prevent the spread of anarchy. Another secret committee was set up to root out any subversive influence. Censorship was rigidly enforced. Gogol's works were not allowed to be re-published. Phrases such as 'sovereign remedy' and 'forces of nature' were removed from textbooks. Almost all foreign fiction was banned, including Hans Christian Andersen's fairy tales. Newspapers were strictly limited in what they could report, especially in terms of foreign news.

The Third Section uncovered the activities of 'The Petrashevsky Circle'. This group was accused of revolutionary conspiracy. In April 1849, 39 members were arrested. But after extensive interrogation and investigation no real evidence of a revolutionary conspiracy could be produced. The 'Circle' had merely met regularly to discuss contemporary problems. In the prevailing atmosphere that was enough. Of those arrested, 21 were sentenced to death. Nicholas determined to make the most out of the case, and staged a dramatic last-second reprieve for the condemned men. An *aide* galloped into Semenovsky Square to announce that the Tsar had decided to exercise clemency and spare their lives, just as the executions were about to take place. This theatrical reprieve was meant to warn of the dangers of revolutionary activity, but at the same time to show how merciful the Tsar was. It had the opposite result. The intelligentsia saw the affair as merely an example of unnecessary cruelty, putting the 21 young men through needless anguish and mental torment merely for effect.

At one stage it looked as if the universities might even be closed down. Uvarov rose to their defence, but the secret committee distrusted his motives and he was persuaded to resign. He was replaced by the utterly subservient Shikmatov, who boasted that 'I have no thought, no will of my own – I am a blind instrument of the will of my sovereign'. The universities were not closed down, but they were strictly controlled in terms of both curriculum and admissions. Student numbers fell by 25 per cent to 3,600 over the next five years. Shikmatov stated that education should be based 'not on reason, but on religious truths connected with theology'.

Censorship increased: by 1850 there were 12 separate bodies with censorship duties. Turgenev was placed under house arrest merely for writing an obituary of Gogol. Even the Slavophiles were refused permission to publish a set of articles putting forward their views, on the grounds that, though they might be suitable for discussion by experts, they might be misinterpreted by a wider audience. This further alienated the intelligentsia, although on the surface all appeared calm.

Abroad, Nicholas succeeded in helping to limit the impact of the 1848 revolutions. He granted a loan of 6 million roubles to help prop up the Austrian regime. He firmly put down a nationalist revolt in Moldavia-Wallachia. In 1849 he sent 150,000 troops into Hungary to help crush the rebellion led by Kossuth. This not only enabled the new Austrian ruler to regain control of Hungary, but also allowed the Austrians to free troops in order to pacify their Italian possessions. In 1850 Nicholas managed to persuade the Prussians to end their plans for a German 'Union' and accept the status quo. Though Russian actions were probably not crucial in stemming the revolutionary movements across Europe, they certainly helped to do so. To many it appeared that Russia alone was stable, and at the peak of her powers.

This illusion was soon shattered by the Crimean War of 1853–6 (see page 116). The real weakness of the Russian Empire was starkly exposed. The army was beautifully prepared for the parade ground, but neither equipped nor prepared to fight a modern war. Russia did not have the necessary industrial and economic base to supply the army properly, and did not have an effective transport system or an efficient bureaucracy to organise and move what supplies there were. The result was ignominious defeat. Nicholas did not survive to see the end of the war. He caught a winter chill but refused to rest and maintained his normal strenuous programme of inspections and work. The strain proved too great and he developed pneumonia and rapidly declined. He died on 18 February 1855. As one commentator recorded: 'A long and, one must admit, a joyless page in the history of the Russian Empire has been written out to the last word.'

6 Assessment

KEY ISSUE In what ways, and for what reasons, was Nicholas I a failure as Tsar?

With the exception of Marxist analysts, historians generally agree on the importance of Nicholas as a strong and determined centralising presence. However, they disagree over what were the most important aspects of his reign: the relative stagnation of the economy, the growth of the bureaucracy, the repression of new ideas, or the deliberate concentration on the policy of 'Orthodoxy, Autocracy, Nationality'. Most opt for the latter on the grounds that this policy embodied all that was negative in Nicholas's reign. Rigid repression did not really grip the country until after 1848, but by then, although Russia appeared strong and vigorous, the real damage had been done. Nicholas gave no positive new direction to the country when it desperately needed it. He sought to improve what existed, but was governed by his fear of new ideas and his belief in the intrinsic values of the old ways and the old system. His reluctance to delegate responsibility led to his taking on so much work himself that his policies could not be implemented adequately. He always tried to see for himself that his wishes were carried out, but in a country of the vast size of Russia this led at best to a superficiality that allowed corruption and inefficiency to grow despite his best efforts. More importantly, his unshakable belief in autocracy and traditional ways prevented Russia from developing.

Nicholas's legacy to his successor was a heavy one. It contained all the problems that had existed on his accession: an increasingly backward economy, an inefficient bureaucracy, an outmoded serf system, a limited education system and a nobility which was moving rapidly towards bankruptcy. However, by the end of his reign these problems had worsened considerably because of the lack of effective action in the face of rapid population growth inside Russia, and the rapid industrial expansion elsewhere. This legacy also contained the developing basis for a police state in the shape of the Third Section, and the basis of a radical opposition in the intelligentsia, who were largely alienated from the Romanov dynasty and increasingly disenchanted with autocracy. Effective change had been held back for 30 years. As the Crimean War showed only too clearly, change was long overdue.

Summary Diagram
Nicholas I 1825–55

1825	The Decembrist revolt	1825

1825	Harsh treatment of the Decembrists Removal of the more reactionary members of the government	1826

1826	Limited reform	1830

1830	The Polish revolt	1830

1830 Arbitrary censorship	Legal reform	1848
Tighter control over education	Economic reform	
Growth of the third section	Reform of the state peasants	
Orthodoxy, autocracy and nationality	Limited serf reform	
The secret committees	Administration improves in some ways	

1848	Rigid repression	1854

1854	The Crimean War	1855

Working on Chapter 3

You need a thorough set of notes on this chapter. The headings, sub-headings and Key Issues should help you. But do not let details obscure your overall understanding. Hence you should focus on what Nicholas wanted to achieve, and on what he did achieve.

Answering structured and essay questions on Chapter 3

The evidence in this chapter should enable you to answer any questions on Nicholas I which do not deal directly with foreign policy. First an example of a stepped question:

a) Why did the Decembrist Revolt fail? (*3 marks*)

b) What methods did Nicholas I use to try to stop political change? (*5 marks*)

c) How successful was Nicholas I in repressing the forces of change during his reign? (*8 marks*)

The third part of a stepped question is often the most taxing. Be sure to ask 'successful' by whose criteria, in what areas, over what time-scale? The last point is very important. What might have appeared to be successful in 1846 might not have still been seen as successful in 1856, 1881 or 1917. Or success in resisting some changes may have been achieved – but at what cost?

Consider also the following essay questions:

I. 'A merely repressive ruler.' Assess the validity of this judgement on Nicholas I's reign.

2. Explain the changes which took place in the internal policies and conditions in Russia between 1825 and 1850.

The first question concentrates on the nature of Nicholas's rule. It asks you to look at his reign and decide whether repression was the only major characteristic of it. Your notes should show you that his reign embodied far more than mere repression. To answer the question you would need to consider the repressive aspects of his reign and show how he might therefore be described as repressive. But you should then go on to consider the other aspects of his reign. These might include his concern over the state peasants and the serfs, his drive for efficiency, his generous treatment of the Finns in contrast to the Poles and the moves towards a balanced budget.

The second question, though using much the same information, asks you to concentrate on the reason for the changes in attitude which took place during Nicholas's reign. This requires you to identify when, if at all, such changes took place, to illustrate the nature of these changes and then to explain their cause. To add depth to your answer you should also consider the idea (even if you reject it) that the whole of his reign can be seen in terms of the often conflicting aims of a desire for progress whilst maintaining the autocracy and traditional Russian values.

You should also be able to tackle a comparative type of question asking you to contrast Alexander I and Nicholas I. An example of this type of question is:

3. Was Nicholas I significantly more repressive than Alexander I?

Construct an essay plan for this question. Remember that it is better to compare the attitudes, policies and actions of the two men directly, rather than having an account of Alexander, followed by a section on Nicholas.

Source-based questions on Chapter 3

1 Nicholas as Tsar

Carefully read the extracts from Nicholas on pages 35 and 45 and from Queen Victoria on page 37. Answer the following questions:

a) What does Nicholas's description of the Decembrist revolt (page 35) reveal about his abilities as Tsar? (*5 marks*)

b) Does Victoria's judgement on Nicholas help to explain any of the problems which he faced during his reign? Explain your answer. (*5 marks*)

c) How revealing is Nicholas's statement to the State Council in 1842 of his overall attitude to reform during his reign? (*5 marks*)

d) Use these extracts and your own knowledge to explain why Nicholas I failed to achieve significant reform in Russia. (*10 marks*)

4 The Emancipation of the Serfs

POINTS TO CONSIDER

This chapter focuses on the Emancipation of the Serfs (1861). Emancipation is often judged to be a relative failure. To evaluate this verdict a number of questions have to be explored. Why did emancipation take place when it did rather than earlier? What were the intended outcomes? What were its unintended outcomes? What happened despite emancipation?

KEY DATES

1855 Death of Nicholas I, accession of Alexander II, while Russian position in the Crimean War was hopeless.
1856 Treaty of Paris ends the war.
1857 Alexander instructs each province to consider reform.
1859 Drafting Commissions appointed to consider proposals.
1861 Emancipation decree; riots by peasants.

1 Alexander II and the Impact of the Crimean War

> **KEY ISSUES** How was Alexander II different from his father? What motivated him? Why did the Crimean War convince Alexander that Emancipation was necessary?

When he came to the throne, in 1855, Alexander II had been prepared for the task, unlike his father. Nicholas had been determined that his son should be fully trained to rule Russia. He had planned his son's education with great care.

Alexander was 37. He had received a broad education, had travelled widely and had been given extensive practical experience in government. He had been the first member of the imperial family to visit Siberia, which gave him some understanding of the conditions suffered by those in exile. He had served on the Council of State for 14 years and on numerous lesser committees, including the secret committees concerned with serfdom and the railways. Alexander had also been left in charge of state affairs on a number of occasions in his father's absence, thus gaining direct experience of the problems of ruling the country. In short, he had a sound knowledge of Russia's problems, a good foundation for the tasks which faced him.

Alexander was rather more humane and sensitive than his father and inspired rather less awe in those around him. Nonetheless he too believed firmly in autocracy as the way forward for his people. He was patriotic, religious and conservative in outlook, but his experience of government had convinced him of the need for change. This was reinforced by the Crimean War. To come to the throne in the midst of the Crimean War, which turned out to be a disastrous defeat, may seem an inauspicious beginning to his reign. Paradoxically, however, it was to aid him in his desire to bring about real change in Russia.

Trotsky once stated that 'War is the Locomotive of History'. If the history of any country supports this view, it must be the history of Russia. After military defeat at the end of the seventeenth century, Peter the Great had almost completely remodelled the Russian state. Catherine the Great had brought in almost equally radical changes under pressure from external events. Now the Crimean War tested the structure of the Russian state and found it wanting. Russia was clearly incapable of competing with the modern European powers. Why was this? A significant clue is given in a message of encouragement from Alexander to his generals, in 1855:

> Do not lose heart; remember 1812 and put your trust in God. Sebastopol is not Moscow and the Crimea is not Russia. Two years after the Moscow fire, our victorious troops were in Paris. We are the same Russians and God is with us.

The last sentence is, ironically, of great importance. Russia in 1855 was indeed virtually the same as Russia in 1812. At the former date she had been backward and, to gain victory, had needed the aid of the Russian winter to destroy half a million of Napoleon's troops. Progress had been made since then, but it was very limited in comparison to the European nations she faced. Comparatively, Russia had gone backwards.

Nicholas died at a time when the Russian position in the Crimea seemed hopeless. Yet the new Tsar did not want his first act to be one of surrender, since this would dishonour the name of Russia. Instead he decided to pursue the war with renewed vigour. At first Russian fortunes did seem to improve, but, at the beginning of September 1855, after 349 days of siege, Sebastopol fell. Alexander II still refused to negotiate and Russia struggled on for a further four months. In the end, however, the threat of Austria joining the war finally forced him to agree to a peace, although not until the day before the Austrian ultimatum expired. Such an ignominious defeat in the war prompted action. For perhaps the first time in Russia, the majority of those with influence felt that some real change was needed. Alexander's first priority was 'Emancipation'.

Defeat in the Crimea affected Alexander deeply. The protection and maintenance of the great Russian state was his primary God-given duty, and it was up to him to restore Russia's prestige and power. He felt that the condition and structure of the Russian peasantry was a crucial factor in Russia's weakness. Both Alexander I and Nicholas I had recognised this before, when they had attempted to address the issue of the serfs, but little significant change had actually been achieved. The Crimean War highlighted the failings in Russian society and once more focused attention upon the problem of serfdom. As a prominent Slavophile (those against westernising Russia), Samarin, noted during the war: 'At the head of our domestic problems which we must tackle stands – as a portent for the future and as an obstacle which precludes at the present time a substantial improvement of anything whatever – the question of serfdom.'

The reason for this conclusion is clear. As late as the middle of the nineteenth century, the Russian peasant was, essentially, Russia. After all, peasants paid most of the taxes, produced the grain which was Russia's most valuable export, produced the food which Russians ate, and formed over 80 per cent of the population. Tolstoy perhaps best characterised the nature of Russia at this time when he described it as a peasant country with a superficial veneer of urban sophistication. Almost half of the peasants were serfs. Their problems were therefore also the problems of the Russian state.

Serfdom was failing on almost all counts. It was failing the serfs themselves, the nobility and the state.

Serfdom was failing the serfs largely because the system was unable to deliver an increasing productivity that matched the rapid population growth. Russia's population doubled between 1800 and 1858 (see page 5). By the 1840s, 30 per cent of the peasants in the north-eastern provinces had to earn their living away from the village. As the population grew, the serfs found their traditional poverty descending to an increasingly intolerable level.

Gambling for souls

Serfdom was failing the nobility in that the system simply no longer provided them with an adequate income to meet their needs in a changing economic climate. The nobility were therefore falling into increasing debt. By 1860, 60 per cent of all private serfs were mortgaged to the state and over 50 per cent of land values were also mortgaged. This weakened the nobility which was one of the foundations of Tsarist rule.

The system was also failing the state because it did not encourage innovation or experiment in both industry and agriculture. This was seen as at least partly responsible for the relative stagnation of the Russian economy in comparison with America and the nations of western Europe. Serfdom no longer even provided stability. With the rapid population growth, the limited amount of land for the peasants to work and the slow increase in productivity, there was often not enough food. This led to a growing tide of unrest. Outbreaks of peasant disobedience, which could be anything from 'insubordination' to full-scale revolt, were rising steadily. Between 1826 and 1834 there were 148 outbreaks; between 1835 and 1844, 216; and between 1845 and 1854, 348.

Alexander thus rightly felt that the serf question was of central importance to the future well-being of the Russian state. The serfs were a key factor in domestic production. They were also the major source of recruits to the army – the same army which had just been so ignominiously defeated. Intent on improving Russia's economic and industrial performance, the Tsar saw the serf system as a major obstacle to progress as the inertia it created stifled innovation and development. The moral aspect of the issue was also of increasing importance as new ideas and standards spread from the west. Coupled with this was the growing threat to the social order of the country as the system increasingly failed to satisfy the basic economic needs of both landlord and serf. Alexander believed that it was his God-given duty to ensure that Russia made progress, grew stronger and became a respected world power again. To accomplish this, the system itself needed to be changed.

2 The Condition of the Peasantry

> **KEY ISSUES** What was life like for Russian peasants? How did their attitudes combine with the situation of the nobility to prevent emancipation up to 1861?

The peasants were divided into two categories: state peasants and landlords' peasants (serfs). Around Moscow and in the western provinces the proportion of serfs was over 50 per cent of the population. The further one moved north, south or east, away from the direct influence of the old Muscovite state, the more state peasants predominated.

a) State Peasants

In theory both groups were bound to the land and could not leave it without permission. In reality, however, the serf was bound to the land, while the state peasant enjoyed varying degrees of freedom. The state peasants were mainly the inhabitants of the Crown Estates (confiscated from the Church in the eighteenth century), or were non-Russians such as Tartars and nomads. They could not leave their village without permission, but they were largely free to indulge in whatever gainful activity they wished as long as they paid their taxes. From 1837 they were able to own land. They did have a large measure of control over their lives, albeit within the peculiar and restrictive confines of the Russian legal system and subject to the whims of the local governors, who were often more responsive to a bribe than to reason and argument.

b) Serfs

Serfs were in a very different position. Their lives were dominated by the *mir*, the family, and the noble who had control over them. The *mir* was a collective unit, which made almost all local decisions over land use and distribution, including when crops should be sown and gathered. Land was normally worked on the 'three field system' (one fallow, with different crops in the other two in rotation) and was normally distributed in strips. Some areas in the village were naturally more fertile than others. To try to ensure a fair distribution of land a family's holding would be made up of strips of land in good and bad areas. Land was also often periodically redistributed as a family's circumstances changed. This may have been fair, but it had a number of serious disadvantages. The strip system led to inefficient use of land, and periodic redistribution tended to discourage serfs from improving the land and adopting innovative techniques. The *mir* (council) was made up of the heads of families and it normally elected one leader or 'Elder'. There was little or no opportunity to appeal against the decision of the council or Elder. Yet for all these defects, most Serfs saw the *mir* as a blessing rather than a burden. It gave them a collective identity, which is captured clearly in the saying: 'a Russian taken individually will not get into heaven, but there is no way of keeping out an entire village'.

The head of the family (normally an extended family of three generations) had almost complete control over the members of the group. He represented their views at the *mir* and had the final say in decisions affecting the family. Sons could not leave home, marry or engage in a trade without permission.

The noble could determine when and to whom his serfs would marry. This usually meant early marriage, as more children were still seen as a way of increasing revenue rather than as an increasing drain on limited resources. He could take serfs into domestic service at will, or indeed ask almost anything else of them, but stories of sexual license and sadistic cruelty were certainly the exception rather than the rule.

Serfs were divided into two categories: those who paid rent (*obrok*) and those who paid in labour (*barschina*). Those who paid *barschina* were, in theory, limited to a maximum of three days' work per week on their lord's land, but they had no one to complain to if this was exceeded. The short length of the summer in much of Russia meant that all the work on their own land and their master's land had to be done in a very limited period. This commonly led to feverish bouts of activity with an 18- or 20-hour day at work, followed by relative idleness during the long winter.

However, those who paid rent (*obrok*) could be just as badly off. They often had some degree of freedom to work at whatever trade they wished, but their masters were known to encourage cottage industry and then vary the rent according to the profits made or their own need. Their need was not always matched by the serfs' productivity. In theory at least, the only action not open to the owner of a serf was murder. There is evidence to suggest that even this occasionally occurred. This wide-ranging power could lead to great misery, as was illustrated by E.N. Vodovosova in her childhood memories of serfdom in Russia:

1　Not far from our estate there was another smaller one belonging to three sisters called Tonchev ... Lala was the favourite; her sisters considered her a beauty, dressed her up, spoiled her, and never gave up hope of seeing her married. With Lala's dowry in mind they tortured
5　their serfs by keeping them at the embroidery frames and looms day and night. The peasants who belonged to the Tonchevs not only had a heavier 'Master's Duty' than was done on other estates, but if the weather was good and Mila's hay not cut they had to work even on 'peasants' days'. This apart, the women had very heavy duties both
10　summer and winter: each had to provide for Lala's dowry a set amount of linen, had to weave with cotton, thread and wool, and had to embroider towels and sheets. In the summer loads of berries and mushrooms had to be gathered for the sisters – and in fact the peasants were so busy all the year round that they had no time left for their own work.
15　Hardly a day passed without someone being whipped by way of punishment: for the smallest fault, offending peasants were beaten by the bailiff in the presence of the two elder sisters ...

Things came to a head in an incident which took place in early autumn when the sisters were on their way home from a party. They were driv-
20　ing in a carriage with the coachman; it was about midnight and very

dark, and they had some three miles of forest to cross. After about a mile they were suddenly surrounded by a crowd; some took the horses by the reins and pulled the coachman down, whilst others pulled the sisters out of the carriage. Lala and the coachman were bound and gagged
25 and dragged to the side of the road whilst Mila and Dia were severely thrashed ... A few months after this incident, the sisters' newly finished house was burnt to the ground. They had already started to pack, ready for the move. This time there was plenty of evidence, but the man who had set fire to the house escaped the same night and was never found.

This was fairly typical of the problems which could and did arise. But these problems were not new.

c) Why did Emancipation Not Come Sooner?

Fear of change and vested interest are key factors. Any real change would have involved loss of land and service for the nobility. Although it is easy to say now that the system was failing them, it is not surprising that the uncertainty over what would, and should, replace serfdom led to inaction. Fear of what change might bring dominated the thinking of the majority, and led to an inertia which was difficult to overcome. There was also an intense desire to avoid what the Russian élite saw as the weaknesses and problems that freedom had brought in western countries. Coupled with this was a very real fear that the autocracy itself might be swept away if such changes were begun.

Another important factor was the attitude of the peasants themselves. At best it can be described as fatalistic. Their horizon barely stretched beyond the village. Indeed, travellers reported that both distance and the existence of other countries outside Russia were barely conceivable to many of them. They did not associate their problems with the Tsar, or with the 'System', but rather with corrupt local officials and landlords. Their anger, when it was occasionally aroused, tended therefore to be directed at something they could comprehend – their immediate local environment. Finally, although their condition was in many ways severe, for the vast majority it was not sufficiently severe to promote outright despair.

The following passage was written by a British traveller in Russia who was far from sympathetic to the idea of serfdom.

1 On the whole ... so far at least as mere food and lodging are concerned, the Russian peasant is not as badly off as the poor man amongst ourselves ... he never knows the misery to which the Irish peasant is exposed ... Not in Ireland only, but in parts of Great Britain usually
5 considered to be exempt from the miseries of Ireland, we have witnessed wretchedness compared with which the condition of the Russian boor is luxury ... Let it not be supposed, however, that, because we admit the Russian peasant to be in many respects more comfortable than our own, we therefore consider his lot as, on the

10 whole, more enviable than that of the peasant in a free country like ours. The distance between them is wide – immeasurable; but it can be accounted for in one single word – the British peasant has rights; the Russian has none!

This was true. However, the concept of 'rights' is very abstract. The majority of Russian peasants neither understood nor were interested in the idea. They did not like to be mistreated, but the threat of starvation was of greater concern. They had suffered both for as long as they could remember. As various groups of revolutionaries were to find to their disappointment over the next 60 years, peasants did not have the time, the inclination, or possibly the conceptual grasp to worry about 'rights'. They were interested in the land and the food it provided – and, in the case of the serfs, in ridding themselves of the burden of the landlords whom they had to support. The serfs' condition limited both their horizons and their perspectives. They had little stake in society and therefore acted as a block to progress on many fronts.

3 The Road to Emancipation

> **KEY ISSUE** How was Alexander II able to introduce emancipation, when his predecessors had failed so completely?

a) Motives

First Alexander used Russia's bitter defeat to underline the need for change. He argued that if Russia was to make economic and social progress, serfdom must end. In this he was helped by the activities of the intellectuals over the preceding 30 years. They had not actually convinced many people, but they had created the intellectual climate in which change of this sort was seen as possibly a positive and progressive move. This feeling had been reinforced by the fact that Nicholas I had repeatedly stated that at some point serfdom must be abolished (see page 45). In addition, Alexander used the growing unrest amongst the serfs to play deliberately on fears of revolution from below. This was successful, though it seems very unlikely that most peasants actually wanted a revolution, or could have grasped such a complex concept. Finally, with these two factors weakening opposition to change, the Tsar was prepared to put the full weight of his autocratic power behind the drive towards emancipation.

Unwittingly, the activities of the serfs helped Alexander in his task. His accession prompted widespread rumours amongst the serfs that emancipation was imminent. Along with this went the feeling, among those serfs who had been drafted into the army during the war, that its end would see them given their freedom. This was normal practice for those who left the army after a full period of service. When neither of these things happened, there was understandable disappointment and unrest.

Alexander addressed the problem in a roundabout way when he announced the peace treaty. He spoke of everyone enjoying 'the fruits of his honest labour, safeguarded by laws equally just and protective for all'. Some hoped that this finally signalled the end of serfdom.

At this crucial point the peasants on the Black Sea coast revolted. For some unknown reason, they became convinced that Napoleon III of France had signed the Treaty of Paris, which ended the Crimean War, on the express understanding that the serfs should be freed. It was further rumoured that the Tsar was waiting at the small town of Perekop in the Crimea to grant freedom to any who presented themselves to him. Thousands set off to meet their 'little father'. Most were turned back at gunpoint. Those who did reach the designated meeting place found only disappointment.

Under previous Tsars these events would have normally led to increased censorship and repression. But Alexander wanted change and took advantage of the situation. Hence he made the following speech to the Moscow nobility, in March 1856:

> For the removal of certain unfounded reports I consider it necessary to declare to you that I have not at present decided to annihilate serfdom; but certainly, as you yourselves know, the existing manner of possessing serfs cannot remain unchanged. It is better to abolish serfdom from
> 5 above than to await the time when it will begin to abolish itself from below. I request you, gentlemen, to consider how this can be put into execution, and to submit my words to the nobility for their consideration ...

b) Drawing Up the Decree

If Alexander hoped for some positive reaction from the nobility, he was to be disappointed. The majority seemed to hope that this Tsar would drop his plans, as his predecessors had done, if only they could delay the decision for long enough. After continued pressure over the next 18 months failed to make any real progress, Alexander finally decided to force the issue. He instructed the Minister of the Interior to produce a plan of action within a week. This plan was published in November 1857. Each province was instructed to form a committee to consider the proposals. Despite their reluctance, they had to accept: an Imperial Rescript (instruction) was not something which could easily be ignored.

In March 1859, the Tsar appointed 'drafting commissions' to examine the comments and proposals of the provincial committees. He appointed General Rostovstev, a close and trusted (if not particularly liberal) friend, to head the commissions. Rostovstev worked closely with the assistant Minister of the Interior, Milyutin, and the Slavophile, Samarin. Rostovstev was persuaded to support emancipation and organised the commissions in a way designed to favour those who wanted change. The proposals fell into two broad categories: those which supported reform and those which did not.

Sympathetic proposals came from 19 provinces. They generally supported emancipation and the distribution of some land to the peasants. In particular they favoured local rather than central administration of the reform. Predictably others were openly critical of reform and attacked Rostovstev and his colleagues for holding dangerously liberal views.

Representatives from the pro-reform provinces were invited to Moscow towards the end of 1859. They were seen in small groups, and gave their views orally. After these views had been considered, the opponents of reform were seen early in 1860. At this point Rostovstev died, and a known reactionary, Panin, was appointed in his place. Many saw this as a clear sign that conservative pressure on the Tsar was having the same effect as it had had on his predecessors. Yet although this pressure existed, it seems likely that Panin's appointment was an astute move to deflect it. Alexander continued to press strongly for reform. The drafting committees worked through the year. Some concessions were made to conservative feeling, but they were relatively minor. Under pressure from Alexander work was finished in October 1860. The Tsar supported the plans personally in the Council of State. This ensured their approval. The Emancipation Ukase (Decree) was published in February 1861. Despite the concessions it retained the spirit of the original proposal.

c) Terms of the Decree

The Decree was long, complex and often obscure. It contained 17 articles and each article contained at least 100 sections. However, the first article was clear: 'the right of bondage' was 'forever abolished'. The serfs were to receive land from the estates of the nobility. In theory they were to receive roughly the same amount of land they had cultivated before emancipation. The State paid compensation to the nobility, and this was to be repaid by the peasants in the form of 'redemption payments'. The *mir* was established as the official organ of self-government. The *mir* held the land collectively and it was collectively responsible for the payment of taxes and redemption dues. It was also responsible for administering justice via special courts. The serfs were now free to enter trade or marry without permission, but they were still subject to a separate system of justice from the rest of Russia.

Emancipation was achieved at last, but there is often a gap between theory and practice. This was such a case. The complexities of the Decree and the way in which it was to be implemented were to cause many problems.

4 Results of Emancipation

> **KEY ISSUES** How far were Alexander's intentions achieved? What
> unexpected reactions and outcomes occurred?

a) Effects on the Peasants

After the enactment of a reform that removed the serfs from the control of the nobility, which they had sought for so long, one might have
expected jubilation from the serfs. But there was little rejoicing. In
the first four months after the Emancipation Decree, there were 647
serious incidents of riot. In 1861 as a whole, there were 499 cases of
riot that needed to be quelled by armed troops. Nor did the peasants
grow much fonder of the terms of the Decree as time passed. That
some landlords were far from content is to be expected, as they lost
land and serfs. But the bitter reaction from the peasants, who
received both freedom and land, needs explanation.

The single most important cause of this discontent was that the
peasants simply could not understand why they were being asked to
pay for land which their families had farmed for generations. As far as
they were concerned, it was theirs by right. Many serfs genuinely
believed that the Tsar had never meant them to pay for what was so
obviously theirs, and that the local landowners were lying to them.
The notion of abstract property rights was something that was largely
beyond their comprehension.

The situation did not improve as the details of land division were
worked out, and the nature of the redemption payments became
known. The division of land was decided at the local level, with the
landlords, who were often in charge of the division, normally retain-
ing the best land for themselves. To buy their land, the peasants had
to make a 20 per cent initial payment, followed by 49 annual 'redemption payments'. These payments included an interest charge. This
might have been feasible if the price fixed for the land had not so
often been grossly inflated above its real worth. The following table
shows how redemption costs varied according to area.

Area	Redemption Cost *Millions of Roubles*	Land Value (Average for 1863–72) *Millions of Roubles*
Black soil provinces	341	284
Non-black soil provinces	340	180
Western provinces	183	184

On average, serfs in the western provinces were charged a 'fair' price
for the land they received. This was not true in other areas. In the

worst cases, in the non-black soil provinces in the north, they were charged twice the land's actual value. Why were there such differences according to area?

The government was far from sympathetic to the Polish landlords in the western provinces, largely because they had long been a thorn in Russia's side with their demands for independence. The relatively few serfs in this area were therefore treated reasonably, as Russia did not have reason to support and protect the landlords who lived there. The significant differences appear in the other two areas. This was partly due to Alexander's wish not to alienate or unduly weaken the nobility, whom the Tsars had relied on for so long as a force for stability. In both these areas Alexander sought to protect the interests of the landlords as he saw them.

In the fertile black soil provinces many landlords were in favour of emancipation. There were two closely connected reasons for this. Firstly, if it could be used efficiently to provide grain for the growing export trade, the land was worth more than the serf's labour. Secondly, many landlords in this area felt that modern methods would lead to significantly increased profits. They wished to move to a system of wage labour in order to introduce these methods. The serfs in these provinces therefore had to pay only a small premium of 15 to 20 per cent above the market value of the land they received. In the provinces to the north, however, the situation was very different. The land had never produced much above subsistence level in terms of food. The peasants had always depended on localised 'cottage industry' to supplement their incomes. The nobility relied heavily on 'rent' rather than labour (*barschina*) to provide their income. This 'rent' was often tied to the 'industrial' production of the serf rather than the value of the land. When it came to compensation for their loss therefore, it was not the value of the land that concerned the nobility so much as the loss of revenue. Thus the serfs found themselves paying almost double the actual value of the land they purchased.

These factors alone would have been enough to cause severe problems, but – with modern farming methods and a new attitude to their relationship to the soil – the ex-serfs might still have overcome these difficulties. However, a group of essentially subsistence peasant farmers cannot be turned into modern agriculturalists at a stroke. Such modernisation required more than just ridding the serfs of their domination by the nobility. It required a radical change in the social and economic structure, and in the attitude of the peasantry towards those structures. The Tsar was not in a position to implement or to offer such a change, even if the peasants had been willing and able to accept it.

The *mir* was not abolished. Indeed it was actually set up in places where it had not existed before, to provide uniformity and a very necessary stability at a time of rapid change. But the *mir* did not allow for the initiative and experiment which both Russia as a whole and the peasantry desperately needed. In economic terms it also often perpetuated many of the worst elements of pre-emancipation Russia. In many places the strip system continued, as did the three field system and periodic land redistribution. These practices positively discouraged innovation, improvement and progress.

The peasants were subject to the *mir* and the special courts based on it. They were still outside the main body of law and functioned, for the most part, according to tradition and custom. The *mir* bound the peasants almost as firmly to their existing lifestyle as their former bondage had done. Where the *mir* had not existed before, its establishment was in some ways actually a backward step. The peasants may have become 'free', but they were still not the equal of other Russian citizens. They remained a class apart, subject to different laws and institutions which offered them fewer rights and less protection than other Russians. The nobility favoured the *mir* because it was collectively responsible for redemption payments. Many peasants favoured the *mir* because it appeared to offer collective security. The problem was that the more progressive elements of the peasantry often found it impossible to withdraw from the collective, thus severely limiting their options, and the collective nature of the *mir* helped to perpetuate old ideas and attitudes.

Coupled with these problems was the unfair distribution of land, not only in terms of quality, but also in terms of quantity. In European Russia the actual acreage held by ex-serfs fell by only about five per cent in the 15 years after 1861. However, in the best black soil provinces of the south, the holdings of ex-serfs fell by about 25 per cent. They also lost many customary rights to woodland and common pasture. This problem was worsened by the continuing and dangerously rapid growth in population, which had doubled between 1800 and 1860. Over the next 40 years it virtually redoubled. In 1858 the population was 68 million; by 1897 it was 125 million.

The standard response of the Russian peasant to the effects of population pressure was to seek more land. Although each individual peasant was free to buy and sell land – and this did take place – there was in a very real sense no more land to be had. The ability to buy and sell land had serious consequences. It led to an increase in the number of landless peasants, who often found it difficult to find alternative employment. It also led to increasing indebtedness amongst the many peasants who, although already in debt, borrowed more money to buy more land.

Yet another problem was that the Emancipation Decree did not come into effect across the country within the two years originally intended. The transitional period, in which ex-serfs still bore a 'temporary obligation' to their former masters, dragged on in many areas of Russia until December 1881, when transfer of lands was finally made compulsory.

Thus for a variety of reasons emancipation failed to transform the peasantry. Redemption payments were too high; the *mir* acted as a brake on innovation and new methods; the industrial base did not expand rapidly enough to attract the growing number of landless peasants; land was frequently apportioned unfairly; and the whole process of land transfer dragged on over decades. The net result was that although productivity had increased by perhaps 20 per cent by the end of the century, this was in effect yet another example of relative stagnation, illustrated by the fact that agricultural productivity more than doubled in Japan during the same period.

b) Effects on the Nobility and the State

Emancipation had a far worse effect on the nobility. For the most part they were totally unprepared for the rigours of existing in a competitive society, without serfs to rely on. Part of the reason for the generous compensation terms they received was that the government wished to ensure their survival as a moderating force in Russian society, in order to counteract more radical groups. Yet emancipation failed to ensure the survival of the nobility. In fact, it hastened their demise. The extra money they received did little good. Half of the money received in the first ten years after 1861 went to pay off existing debts. By 1905 they had been forced to sell one-third of the land they had kept in 1861. Of the land they still retained in 1905, over 50 per cent was mortgaged in some fashion. Though there were a few notable exceptions, particularly in the Ukraine and Georgia, a large proportion of the nobility simply could not make their estates pay. They therefore declined steadily, as did their ability to act as a stabilising force in Russian society. The position and power of the nobility had been based on serfdom. Emancipation effectively condemned them as a class.

Perhaps the most important initial motivation for introducing emancipation was the desire to strengthen the Russian state – in military, economic and industrial terms. It was hoped that a revitalised peasant economy would provide the basis for industrialisation by providing surplus capital for investment. The combined effect of the failings noted above was that this aim was not achieved. Money was taken from the agricultural sector, but very little was put back in to encourage new methods and higher productivity. One can argue that agriculture was bled dry in order to finance industrialisation, but that the move was counter-productive in that the lack of investment in agriculture meant that it could not provide enough capital to finance effective industrialisation. Russia did of course make progress, but not when compared with the rapidly growing economies of western Europe. In comparative terms she was still falling further and further behind her competitors. New tensions were thus introduced into Russian society without achieving the central aim of the reform. We see the impact of these tensions in later chapters.

5 Assessment

KEY ISSUE Should the limited nature of Emancipation be condemned?

Almost all historians agree that the Emancipation Decree was a momentous event in Russian history, that it was of great importance and that it failed to achieve its aims. But there is considerable disagreement over the precise reasons for this failure. Part of the criticism appears to be generated by the search for causes of the 1917 revolution. That search has sometimes led to emancipation being assessed more in terms of Russia in 1917 than of Russia in 1861. In an attempt to find a 'convenient' cause of the momentous events of 1917, it seems that some historians may have been overly eager to lay the blame for the revolution, at least partly, on the shortcomings of emancipation.

Richard Pipes (see Further Reading) characterises emancipation as being too cautious, too little and too late. With the benefit of hindsight, it is possible to have sympathy with this argument in terms of Russian history in general. But a consideration of the problems faced by Alexander seems to suggest that it is a little unfair to him. Previous tsars could certainly have been more determined in their attempts to modernise Russia, but Alexander could hardly have acted with greater speed. If we dismiss the idea of 'too late' in terms of Alexander on the basis that he could hardly have acted sooner, we are left with 'too cautious' and 'too little'.

There is no doubt that 'redemption payments' were too heavy for the majority of ex-serfs to bear. But Alexander could not have been deliberately expected to destroy the nobility. He wanted them as a stabilising influence in post-emancipation Russia. It is clear also that the lack of full civil rights and the continuance of the *mir* proved to be significant blocks to progress. Yet what was the alternative? The nobility were clearly not appropriate people to continue to control the peasants. As for state administration, that was notorious for its corruption. Indeed one of the chief complaints of the state peasants was the corruption of the local officials. A modern democratic alternative was certainly not on offer. So it would seem that allowing the peasants to run their own affairs at this time via a traditional, popular and trusted institution was a reasonable course of action.

The key to understanding the effects and success/failure of emancipation is to see them in the context of the other problems facing Russia. These problems might have been overcome if the Tsar had been prepared to abandon autocracy, but he was not. As Alexander emphasised in 1865 over another area of reform, he still believed firmly in the principle of autocracy. He still believed that he derived power from 'God Himself'. As with Alexander I before him, Alexander II found it difficult to be a reforming autocrat. His basic motivation was to make Russia strong and to serve his people, not to be a liberal reformer. He did not believe that Russia would benefit from liberal reforms and it would be simplistic to condemn Alexander for this stance. In political, social and economic terms, Russia in 1861 was still a backward nation. There is every reason to suppose that had any more radical reform been imposed from above, the Russian state would have collapsed into anarchy and chaos. The fact that emancipation still left the Empire far behind much of Europe should not obscure the very real and very dramatic impact it had on contemporary Russia.

No such attempt at change, even one backed by an imperial decree, can transform a large society at a stroke. Even if one does not consider emancipation, Alexander did bring about a surprising, indeed an almost revolutionary, degree of reform and change (see pages 74–86). The outcome of emancipation depended, to a large degree, on these other reforms. They were necessarily dependent on each other for their success or failure. The next two chapters will consider the nature and impact of these other areas of reform. If they had been more successful, emancipation, with all its faults, might also have been more successful.

Summary Diagram
The Emancipation of the Serfs

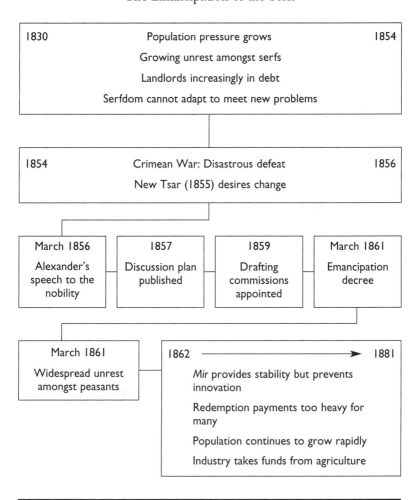

1830	Population pressure grows	1854
	Growing unrest amongst serfs	
	Landlords increasingly in debt	
	Serfdom cannot adapt to meet new problems	

| 1854 | Crimean War: Disastrous defeat | 1856 |
| | New Tsar (1855) desires change | |

| March 1856 | 1857 | 1859 | March 1861 |
| Alexander's speech to the nobility | Discussion plan published | Drafting commissions appointed | Emancipation decree |

March 1861	1862 ———————————————→ 1881
Widespread unrest amongst peasants	*Mir* provides stability but prevents innovation
	Redemption payments too heavy for many
	Population continues to grow rapidly
	Industry takes funds from agriculture

Working on Chapter 4

You need to understand why emancipation took place, what its terms were, the effects it was supposed to have and the effects it did have. Bear in mind that Alexander II wanted progress but not liberal progress. Look at the summary diagram. Can you show how each element in the first two boxes were causal elements, how those in the next four played a part in bringing about emancipation, and how those in the final two comprise intended or unintended outcomes? Consider whose expectations emancipation satisfied.

Answering structured and essay questions on Chapter 4

You will need to use much of the information in this chapter to answer the more general questions on Alexander's reforms discussed on page 87. You are also likely to be asked to answer specific questions on emancipation. These questions will concentrate on causes, consequences, or both.

An example of the first type of question would be:

1. Why did emancipation take place in Russia in 1861?

The question is a straightforward 'Why?' Plan your answer by following these steps:

a) Make a list of about six reasons why emancipation took place in 1861, for example because Alexander wanted to strengthen Russia (make sure that you explain the ways in which he wanted to strengthen Russia).
b) List the evidence you would use to back up your statements.
c) Decide on their order of importance.

Be careful how you decide on their order of importance. Would the order be different for example if the question was:

2. 'Why did Alexander II emancipate the serfs in 1861?', or
3. 'Why was the Crimean War followed by emancipation?'

The second type of question might be:

4. What were the consequences of emancipation during the reign of Alexander II?

Here you could again repeat the exercise above and list the major ways in which it did fail, with evidence to illustrate the nature and importance of failure in the areas you choose. Again, however, remember to avoid a completely one-sided approach. Include at least some reference to the positive aspects of emancipation. You should return to this question after reading Chapters 6 and 7, to decide what information on other aspects of Alexander's reign might usefully be included.

An example of the combined question would be:

5. Why, and with what results during his reign, did Alexander II emancipate the serfs in Russia?'

Source-based questions on Chapter 4

1. Serfdom

Study carefully the engraving by Doré on page 57 and read the extracts from Vodovosova's memoirs on pages 60–61 and from the British traveller on pages 61–2. Answer the following questions:

a) Identify (by type) i) the people bound together on the table and ii) the card players. (*2 marks*)

b) What message is the artist attempting to communicate? (*3 marks*)

c) What does the extract from Vodovosova tell us about the control the landlords had over the lives of the serfs? (*2 marks*)

d) How did the serfs take revenge on the Tonchevs? Why did they adopt this particular approach? (*3 marks*)

e) Why did the British traveller refer to 'the Russian boor' (page 61 line 7)? (*2 marks*)

f) In what ways does the serf's life portrayed by the Briton differ from that given by Vodovosova? (*5 marks*)

g) What does the final sentence tell us about the perspective of the British author? Does this perspective lessen the value of this extract as evidence about serfdom? (*4 marks*)

h) Use your knowledge to explain how complete a picture of the life of the Russian serfs these sources provide. (*6 marks*)

5 The Reforming Tsar

POINTS TO CONSIDER

Alexander II wanted a strong and stable Russia. This chapter looks at the reforms he implemented. Serfdom had in many ways been the cornerstone of autocratic Russia. After emancipation, the issue was not whether there would be other reforms, but rather when and what form they would take. Alexander was convinced that in order to maintain stability and achieve his aim of a strong Russian state, he needed to transform much of the existing social and political system. He pushed through reforms in almost all areas of life: local government, the legal system, the military, education, censorship and the economy. Without the strong personal pressure he exerted in favour of reform, much of it would not have taken place. You need to consider how far these reforms were radical, thorough and effective. Could further change have been implemented? If so, would it have had positive results, and for whom?

KEY DATES

1859 Length of service in army reduced.
1861 Beginning of expansion of schools.
1862 Public Budget set and published; new schools now under Ministry of Education; regional military commands established.
1863 Universities given significant autonomy; end of more extreme forms of punishment in Army; village officials now appointed by state.
1864 *Zemstva* established.
1865 Press given greater freedom.
1872 First women admitted to Moscow University.
1874 Conscription extended to all; length of military service reduced.

1 Local Government

> **KEY ISSUES** What was Alexander trying to achieve? How far did he succeed? What was he not prepared to risk in order to achieve his aims?

The development of local government is typical of Alexander's attitude to reform. At his accession there was effectively no elected local government. He felt that this lack contributed significantly to administrative inefficiency and therefore determined to remedy the situation. Yet he was equally determined that it should not appear that it was being forced upon him. He firmly suppressed public calls for reform.

In 1859, whilst discussing the terms of emancipation, nobles from the Tver province went too far in Alexander's eyes. They called for an independent judiciary, some form of local government independent of the bureaucracy, and an elected body to deal with economic affairs. Their spokesman, Unkovsky, was promptly sent into exile. In 1862, 13 nobles from Tver called for an elected and classless national assembly. They were imprisoned in St Petersburg. Alexander was not prepared to countenance a national assembly, nor open debate on the matter. He was nevertheless determined that reform of local government would take place. The commission which he had set up in 1861 had still produced no firm proposals towards the end of 1863. In November, he therefore instructed the commission to finish its task by the end of the year. The decree establishing the *zemstva* was duly published in January 1864.

The *zemstva* (singular *zemstvo*) were local elected councils. The powers given to them reflect the nature of the struggle which was taking place between the liberals and the more reactionary elements in Russia. The liberals wanted the councils to have real power and in part they succeeded. The *zemstva* were given responsibility for public education, public health, local economic development, road building and the provision of services such as water and fire prevention. The liberals also wanted them to be given power over the disposal of imperial taxes, but in this they failed. This failure shows the division which existed between the desire for reform and the equally strong desire to maintain autocratic control. The argument was clearly put by Valuev, the conservative Minister of the Interior appointed in 1861. He stated that:

1 To give the zemstva a voice in matters common to the whole empire would be to break up the unitary executive power of the empire and distribute it among some forty or fifty bodies. This would expose the social order and the entire imperial structure to perils which must be
5 apparent to everyone.

Alexander wanted reform, he wanted to devolve some power from the centre, but he also wished to remain in firm control and to maintain stability. It was felt that giving the *zemstva* control over imperial finance would undermine those aims.

The membership of the *zemstva* also reflected the desire of the conservative elements and the Tsar to retain the nobility as a bulwark against undue radicalism. The *zemstva* were two-tiered: district *uezd* and provincial *gubernia*. The seats for the district *zemstva* were divided amongst the three classes: 45 per cent to the nobility, 40 per cent to the peasants and 15 per cent to the townsmen and the clergy. These district *zemstva* then elected representatives to the provincial level. The system was designed to ensure that no one grouping had overall control. At the local level this succeeded, but it is easy to see why the nobility tended to dominate at the provincial level.

The *zemstva* did not treat all groups equally. Local taxation continued to favour the nobility rather than the peasantry, but by virtue of their local knowledge, the *zemstva* did improve local administration in the areas in which they were allowed to operate. The following comments written by Sir Mackenzie Wallace, who lived in Russia from 1870 to 1875, is representative of the 'objective' assessments which have come down to us:

1 What surprised me most in this [*zemstvo*] assembly was that it was composed partly of nobles and partly of peasants … and that no trace of antagonism seemed to exist between the two classes. Landed proprietors and their ci-devant [former] serfs, emancipated only ten years before, evi-
5 dently met for the moment on a footing of equality. The discussions were carried on chiefly by the nobles, but on more than one occasion peasant members rose to speak, and their remarks, always clear, practical, and to the point, were invariably listened to with respectful attention …
    The *zemstvo* … fulfils tolerably well without scandalous speculation
10 and jobbery, its commonplace, every-day duties … It has done a very great deal to provide medical aid and primary education for the common people, and it has improved wonderfully the condition of hospitals, lunatic asylums, and other benevolent institutions committed to its charge. In its efforts to aid the peasantry it has helped to improve the
15 native breeds of horses and cattle, and it has created a system of obligatory fire insurance, together with means for preventing and extinguishing fires in the villages – a most important matter in a country where the peasants live in wooden houses and big fires are fearfully frequent.

In 1870, a Municipal Statute set up a similar system in the towns. A town council - *duma* - was elected by Russian male property holders over the age of 25. These councils too were given responsibility for public health, provision of services, roads, public education and local trade and industry. The one key area they were not given control over was the police. Their function was one over which the imperial government was determined to keep firm control.

It has been argued, both by historians and contemporary critics, that the success of the *zemstva* showed how capable the 'people' were of looking after themselves, and that it was short-sighted and indeed tragic that the representative principle was not extended to central government. This argument has merit, but it does not lessen the significance of the establishment of the *zemstva*. At the local level at least, representation was now much broader than in many supposedly advanced western countries.

2 Legal Reform

> **KEY ISSUES** Did the legal reforms address important issues? Were they effective and what unintended consequences did they have?

The judicial reform introduced in 1864 was as important as local government reorganisation. The Russian judicial system was sorely in need of change. There were numerous different types of court, and officials were often ill-trained and illiterate. Evidence was normally written, the accused rarely saw the judges, and the written evidence of the nobility was usually given more credence than that from any other group. Corruption was rife and cases often dragged on for years, as vividly expressed in the proverb: 'No grease, no motion'.

The reform of 1864 was intended to sweep away all the old abuses and to set up a system which was not only fair and just, but was seen to be so. As the Tsar himself put it in his decree to the senate:

1 On ascending to the throne of my ancestors, one of my first wishes publicly proclaimed in the manifesto of 19 March 1856, was: 'May justice and mercy reign in our courts!' Ever since that time, amidst other reforms called for by the needs of our national life, I have never ceased
5 to reflect on the manner of achieving this object through a better organisation of the judiciary ...

   [These statutes are intended] ... to establish in Russia expeditious, just, merciful, and impartial courts for all our subjects; to raise the judicial authority by giving it proper independence and, in general, to
10 increase in the people that respect for the law which national well-being requires, and which must be the constant guide of all and everyone from the highest to the lowest.

This is almost exactly what the reform did. To avoid bribery, salaries were set deliberately high. Trials became public, trial by jury was introduced and appeal courts were set up. It was now expected that oral evidence would be presented and cross-examined in open court. There were two tiers to the system. Justices of the Peace were elected by the district *zemstva* for a period of three years; and Judges were nominated to the regular courts by the Tsar. Once they were appointed they were virtually guaranteed independence as it was very difficult to remove them.

Mackenzie Wallace was in no doubt as to the effectiveness of the new system. He stated that:

1 In the Justice of Peace Courts ... the Justice, always scrupulously polite without the distinction of persons, listened patiently to the complaint, tried to arrange the affair amicably, and when his efforts failed, gave his decision at once according to the law and common sense. No attention
5 was paid to rank or social position ... No wonder such courts became popular among the masses; and their popularity increased when it became known that the affairs were disposed of expeditiously, without unnecessary formalities and without any bribes or blackmail.

This might seem too rosy a picture to believe. However, if further evidence is needed that the judiciary and the juries took seriously their freedom to operate, one has only to examine the Vera Zasulich case in 1878 (see page 95). In this case, an admitted revolutionary who had shot General Trepov was found not guilty against all the evidence and the express wishes of the Minister of Justice.

Of course, this case points to some idiosyncrasies in the system. Firstly, the authorities could still use powers of administrative arrest and special courts for certain crimes. After the Zasulich case the authorities never again relied on the regular courts to deal with terrorist activity. It also points to the fact that juries often acted as they felt it right to act, rather than as the evidence suggested they should. There were set sentences for certain crimes, but juries found a way round this restriction. In more than one case it is recorded that juries, upon being asked 'Do you find the accused guilty to the charge of horse-stealing?' replied firmly: 'Yes, the accused is found guilty of stealing rabbits.' Thus the jury reduced the severity of the sentence whilst admitting the guilt of the accused.

Nor was this attitude restricted to the juries. Wallace records that the Justices often carried their sense of duty to what might to us appear to be extremes. Sometimes they 'took a malicious delight in wounding the susceptibilities, and occasionally even the material interests, of those whom they regarded as enemies of the good cause'. Yet such cases were not common. They became even less so as it was realised that the judiciary was, by and large, independent and fair. Attempts deliberately to misuse the system declined rapidly, while the efficiency of the courts rose dramatically. Three times as many cases as the authorities had anticipated were heard. The courts became trusted and gained the confidence and respect of all social groups – except perhaps the conservative élite.

There was another consequence that had not been anticipated. Open and efficient courts needed trained lawyers and judges. The Tsar agreed to the setting up of an independent bar. This led to the growth of a body of people, trained in the art of persuasion, fully conversant with officialdom and the law, and generally disposed towards liberal ideas. Such a body required freedom to debate and discuss ideas. It proved to be the ideal breeding ground for reformers, some of whom were to become prominent revolutionaries in the future. The creation of this 'dangerous' group was not the intention of the judicial reforms, but it was a necessary by-product.

3 Military Reform

> **KEY ISSUE** Why was the Russian military machine reformed, and with what success?

The Crimean War had shown all too clearly the shortcomings of the Russian military system. Despite the fact that the army consumed almost one-third of the government's income, it had failed to defeat inferior numbers of foreign troops on Russian territory. Though this was partly due to problems of transportation, it also pointed to other serious problems.

The command structure and the administration were inflexible and inefficient. Punishment was often severe and barbaric. The period of service for conscripts was 25 years (often viewed as a life sentence), and those who could avoided military service in any way possible. To make matters worse, performance on the parade ground was normally regarded more highly than the ability to fight.

In 1861 the Tsar appointed Miliutin as Minister of War, with the explicit task of reforming the military. Miliutin held office for the next 20 years. He was an able administrator who took a keen interest in all affairs of state and generally took a liberal stance on most issues. Though often strongly opposed by conservative elements in the government and the army, he enjoyed the enthusiastic support of the Grand Duke Constantine, the Minister of the Marine. This imperial support often helped him through turbulent waters.

Miliutin sought to humanise the military and improve its efficiency in all aspects. He set about his task with considerable vigour. In 1862, regional commands were set up in four areas. The aim was to improve efficiency by decentralising administration and supply. In 1864, six further regional commands were established. In 1863 the more extreme forms of corporal punishment were ended and the Military Code was revised. Miliutin also set about reducing the influence of the old cadet corps, which until now had produced the officers of the army. He set up special army schools (*Junker* schools) which were open to all. This was a significant step forward, and by 1871 12 per cent of the *Junker* students were not from the nobility. This was an important advance away from privilege and patronage, and towards promotion and selection on merit. The compulsory length of service for conscripts had already been reduced from 25 to 16 years in 1859. Plans were laid to further reduce the length of, and to extend the liability to, service. This was intended to make the army a less fearsome prospect and to prevent people avoiding military service.

These reforms generated antagonism amongst the traditionalists in the army and amongst the conservative elements in the government. The nobility, reeling from the shock of the numerous reforms that were undermining their rights and position, closed ranks against the idea that their sons should be treated equally with the sons of their former serfs. It began to look as if they would prevent Miliutin's plans for further reform from being put into practice. However, the striking success of the Prussian army against the French in 1870–71 gave Miliutin the lever he needed. It showed what could be achieved by a modern army that was efficiently organised and led. Using the Prussian example as a model, he was able to force his reforms through.

In 1874, the Manifesto and Statute on Universal Military Service was published. It became law in 1875. Liability to military service and conscription were extended to all classes. The hiring of substitute conscripts was forbidden. Service in the army was no longer an

optional punishment for criminals. All males upon reaching 21 years
of age had to register. About one-quarter of these were chosen by lot
to serve. Only those unfit for service were exempted – though in practice deferments on compassionate grounds were obtainable for all
classes. Service was limited to 15 years, with normally only about seven
spent on active service. Length of service was significantly reduced for
those who volunteered and for those with an education. University
graduates, for example, only had to serve six months on active service.
Even those with merely a primary education had to serve only four
years. Though these reductions obviously favoured the educated (and
therefore the nobility and the rich over the peasantry) it was still a
major step forward in social as well as military terms. In the area of
conscription at least, the son of the lowest peasant was now theoretically treated in exactly the same manner as the son of the highest
noble.

This change was not inevitable. Miliutin's diary provides a clear
and fascinating insight into the bitter in-fighting which went on
throughout 1873. Indeed as the year drew to a close, he seemed closer
to despair than to reaching a cherished goal:

1   December 31, 1873. On the last day of the year my thoughts turn back
    and quickly run through a whole series of impressions preserved in my
    memory. For me the year 1873 passed by as a dark shadow; it leaves
    behind none but melancholy impressions. Not in a single preceding year
5   have I endured so much unpleasantness, sorrow and failure. The
    intrigue against me, begun long since, has fully matured and has broken
    out in all its vileness. My enemies have not succeeded in fully attaining
    their aims; they cannot consider themselves victorious but have
    nonetheless managed to injure me in the eyes of the sovereign and to
10 make my position within the government almost impossible ... As for
    general affairs of state which lie outside the sphere of the military
    department, in this respect I have been entirely set aside. Everything is
    done under the sole influence of Count Shuvalov [Head of the Third
    Section 1866–74], who has alarmed the sovereign by his daily reports
15 on the fearful dangers to which both the state and the sovereign are
    said to be exposed ... He has surrounded the sovereign with his own
    supporters; all new appointments are made in accordance with his
    directions. In this way, by now the majority of members in the
    Committee of Ministers always act in unison with Count Shuvalov, the
20 way an orchestra follows the baton of its conductor...

There can be little doubt that in the face of such opposition only the
support of the Tsar could have enabled Miliutin to force reform
through. Alexander put his full weight behind enabling Miliutin to do
so. He felt strongly that the defence of 'the fatherland' was a common
concern to all his subjects. He saw it as his 'sacred task', and the 'sacred
task' of all Russians, to ensure that Russia was able to defend herself.
Put in these terms, there were few who dared oppose his view.

One can argue that this reform was the most 'democratic' in its implications of all the reforms carried out under Alexander II. It treated all Russians equally, excepting the reference to education. However, it was not a complete success. The General Staff, although improved, were still burdened with far too many regulations and diverse tasks. Not until 1900 was it finally agreed that their duties should be clearly laid down – and even then this had not come into operation before the Russo-Japanese War began in 1904. Army doctors could still be bribed to declare people unfit for service. The quality of training and leadership still lagged far behind that of the Prussians. Yet great improvements were made, and their effects could clearly be seen in the improved performance of the army in the Russo-Turkish War of 1878.

4 Education

> **KEY ISSUE** What level of compromise was reached between the wish for educational reforms and the desire to retain autocratic control?

Until 1861 strict and repressive control was maintained over education. Then Alexander appointed Golvonin as Minister of Education. He, like Miliutin, was a close colleague of Grand Duke Constantine and was most definitely aligned with the liberal reformers.

Golvonin set out at once to reform the education system. It was decided to develop primary education in the villages. The task was soon handed over to the *zemstva*. The *duma* later carried out a similar task in the towns. Both were encouraged to expand primary education. Between 1861 and 1881 the number of primary and secondary schools increased fourfold. In 1862 new schools were placed under the jurisdiction of the Ministry of Education rather than under the control of the Church. This was intended to free them from the traditionally stifling influence of the Church. New schemes of work were developed and prizes were offered for the best textbooks produced. Significant progress was made in terms of both the quality of the education provided and pupil numbers.

The University Regulations of 1863 were Golvonin's most famous contribution to the education system, although perhaps they were of no greater impact than his work with primary and secondary schools. These regulations changed the basis of university activity. They allowed a freedom of expression which had certainly not been seen for 50 years. The universities were given virtual autonomy in administrative matters and, although the curriculum was prescribed by the Ministry, much greater freedom was allowed in terms of presentation and treatment. Rectors were appointed for four years by a Council of Professors. Deans were elected by faculties for three years. The teaching of law was upgraded, and in the case of constitutional law was actually reinstated. This was a major change. However, perhaps the most far-reaching of the regulations are set out below. They point to a radical change in stance and attitude towards the liberty and needs of both the individual and the group within Russian society.

The University Regulations of 18 June 1863

90. Besides students, outsiders are also permitted to attend lectures ...

107. For the relief of needy students, the Universities are allowed to grant deferments of payment, or to reduce it by as much as one-half, or even to waive it entirely ...

114. Academic degrees may be obtained both by Russian subjects and by foreigners ...

129. Universities are accorded the right to import, at liberty and duty free, scholarly texts of any kind from abroad ...

130. Books, manuscripts, and periodical publications that the universities receive from foreign countries are not subject to examination by the censorship.

Alexander took a close personal interest in the drafting of the Regulations and in the promotion of the universities. Scholarships were set up to support the best students. Fact-finding expeditions abroad were encouraged. The universities began to flourish in the new atmosphere of open enquiry.

An incident in 1866 prevented this atmosphere from continuing to develop unchecked. A former student of Kazan University attempted to assassinate the Tsar. This was the excuse Golvonin's opponents had sought. A commission appointed to investigate the attempt attributed it to the growth of radical ideas fostered by the newly relaxed and liberal education policies. Golvonin was replaced by the much more conservative Dmitri Tolstoy. Although Tolstoy restricted entry to the universities somewhat, and placed some disciplinary powers in the hands of the police rather than the university authorities, he did not seriously interfere with the foundation laid down by Golvonin. The universities continued to flourish until the end of Alexander's reign.

Yet Tolstoy's impact was greater in other areas. In 1871 he introduced a new 'classical' curriculum into the *gymnasia* (higher secondary schools). Great emphasis was placed on the study of Greek, Latin and mathematics. The same law also gave power to the Ministry to dictate curricula in schools and to control appointments, as well as making graduation considerably more dependent upon rote learning. In 1872 Tolstoy took similar powers over the modern technical schools (*realschule*), whilst at the same time increasing their number. He also made it a condition of entry to the universities that students had graduated from a *gymnasium*. At the same time new technical institutes were set up for students from the *realschule*. This meant that they could continue their studies without being exposed to the possibly corrupting influence of the universities.

Russian liberals saw these measures as unreservedly reactionary in nature, designed merely to prevent the spread of modern knowledge. This feeling was doubtless strengthened by Tolstoy's close links with the Orthodox Church. Nevertheless, students from district schools were enabled to go on to *gymnasia*. Though the intent of the reforms may have been repressive, the actual effect was not that severe. Indeed there were positive aspects in terms of administrative efficiency and equality of opportunity. Positive steps were also made in other areas, albeit without Tolstoy's active support. Women's education made great strides. 1872 saw Moscow University organise the first courses for women. Women were also admitted to the Medical Academy in St Petersburg. After an Imperial Statute in 1876, five universities set up degree courses for women. By 1881 there were some 2,000 women studying at universities in Russia.

Again, therefore, we see an uneasy balance being struck between progressive liberal initiatives and a desire to maintain control of events. The Tsar first appointed a liberal, Golvonin, to bring in radical changes to the educational system. Once these initiatives were firmly in place (and admittedly under pressure from conservative advisers) he appointed a conservative figure, Tolstoy, to keep the effects of these changes in check. However he did not allow Tolstoy actually to undo Golvonin's work. Then and now, critics have argued that this merely gave the Tsar and Russia the worst of all worlds, and that what was needed was continuing and thoroughgoing reform. But the Tsar did not want revolution. He felt that it was his duty to maintain his position. As we shall see below, he had every reason to beware. More change had been thrust upon Russia in ten years than had taken place in the previous 150 years. The results were bound to be somewhat unsettling. He was determined not to allow the situation to develop to the point where it could no longer be controlled.

5 Censorship

> **KEY ISSUE** Does this period mark a significant change in the application of censorship?

As seen above (pages 46–7), the censorship laws under Nicholas I were extremely complex, and could be very harsh. After Alexander's accession the situation relaxed for a time, but when, in 1863, responsibility for censorship was passed to Valuev, the Minister of the Interior, the system again became tighter. The duality of the Tsar's approach to reform is shown by the fact that once censorship had been tightened, the relatively progressive Press Laws were published in 1865. Some of the key elements of these laws are given below:

Freed from preliminary censorship are:

A In both capitals:
1. All currently issued periodical publications, if their publishers shall themselves state this desire.
2. All original writings of not less than 160 printed pages in length.

B Everywhere:
All government publications.
All publications of academics, universities, and learned societies and institutions.
3. All publications in the ancient classical languages and translations from those languages.
4. Sketches, diagrams and maps.

IV. Everyone who wishes to issue a new periodical publication in the form of a newspaper, magazine or anthology is obliged, now as before, to obtain permission of the minister of internal affairs.

XXVIII. The minister of internal affairs is accorded the right to issue warnings to periodical publications, indicating the articles giving cause for this. A third warning suspends publication for a period of time designated by the minister ... but not exceeding six months ...

Although the detested preliminary (pre-publication) censorship was largely abolished, the statute retained teeth with which to work. Critics argue that censorship remained strict. It is true that several papers received warnings within the first few weeks. It is also true that in 1866 the radical journal *The Contemporary* was prohibited. However, the former seems to have been by nature of a warning not to go too far, and the latter occurred in the wake of the attempt on the Tsar's life. Censorship was strict by modern British standards, but in comparison to what had gone before in Russia it represented a considerable increase in freedom of both ideas and expression. The number of new books which were published per year doubled between 1855 and 1864, and trebled between 1864 and 1881. It was not until the last few years of Alexander's reign that censorship really began to bite hard again, and even then it was not nearly as severe as it had been under Nicholas I. There was a change in the relationship between publisher and censor: a mood of cooperation rather than repression prevailed.

6 Economic Reform

> **KEY ISSUES** What was the main objective of economic reform? Were these reforms pragmatic rather than ideological?

Reutern was appointed Minister of Finance in 1862, and continued in office until 1878. He created a unified Treasury and introduced an efficient centralised administrative system. After 1862 budgets were published, and in 1863 a system of excise duties replaced the medieval system of farming out licences to sell certain goods, especially spirits, which were still a key source of revenue. He modernised and streamlined the fiscal organisation of the state.

Of greater importance were the moves to stimulate the Russian economy. A great deal of effort was expended on establishing a railway network. When Alexander II came to the throne there were less than 700 miles of track laid. By 1881, there were over 14,000 miles of track. This was achieved by initially guaranteeing the annual dividend on shares of investors, especially those from abroad who were uncertain as to the reliability of the investment. Much of the new railway system was designed to encourage grain exports, which were Russia's chief source of foreign revenue. This was a great success. In 1864, exports stood at approximately 26 million tons. By 1880 they had risen to 86 million tons.

Of almost equal importance was the effort made to develop and expand Russia's financial institutions. In 1855 the majority of Russians still relied on moneylenders to service their needs. By 1878 there were 278 municipal banks, 727 loan and savings associations, 566 joint-stock companies and 33 joint-stock commercial banks. Much of this explosion was the result of Reutern's sound administration and encouragement. Russian industry had long suffered from the fact that it was very difficult to raise money for investment and expansion. This growth of the financial institutions did not solve the problem, but it did much to alleviate it.

Virtually nothing was ignored which might assist economic expansion. Jews in Russia had lived under strict rules about what trade they could practise and where they could live. Up to 1855 they were restricted to living in the border regions – the 'Pale of Settlement'. It was realised that these restrictions meant that the Jews could not make a full contribution to the Russian economy. Under Alexander II, many of the more onerous restrictions were lifted. In 1859 Jewish merchants of the First Guild (those who paid above a certain amount in taxes) and all foreign Jews were allowed to live and trade throughout the Empire. In 1860 this right was extended to all Jews who had served in certain regiments, and in 1867 to all Jews who had been soldiers. Perhaps the most important move, and certainly the most significant was the *Policy on Jewish Artisans* issued in 1865. This law abolished the 'pale' for Jewish artisans.

The importance of this move lies in the motivation behind it. Antisemitism still prevailed. Indeed some forms of restrictive legislation (the closing of many Jewish schools and the limiting of Jewish representation) increased after 1863. So, the motivation lay for the most part not in any view of what was right and just, but in what made good economic sense. This is clearly shown by the following note from the Minister of the Interior to the Tsar in 1865:

1 The reason for the decline of the handicraft industry among the Jews must be sought in the general limitations upon the civil rights of this people ... and most of all in the prohibition upon Jewish residence outside the regions designated for their settlement.

5 From information in the possession of Internal Affairs it is clear that those who suffer most from this limitation on the rights of Jews to live outside the pale ... are the artisans, Christian as well as Jewish ...

In keeping with these convictions the Ministry of Internal Affairs considers that Jewish artisans should immediately be accorded the opportunity to reside outside their pale of settlement. There is no doubt that such permission would be advantageous in every respect.

As with the other areas discussed in this chapter and with emancipation, the results, whatever the motive, were considerable compared with what had gone before. Progress was not always smooth as there were many complex interacting forces at work, but progress there most certainly was. One might be forgiven for expecting, as Alexander almost certainly did, that public reactions would be favourable. In general terms initial reactions were usually supportive. But the reaction of the intelligentsia was far from favourable. This was important because the intelligentsia were the opinion leaders of their day, and their views were beginning to count. In the next chapter we examine the reasons for this apparently strange response.

Summary Diagram
The Reforming Tsar

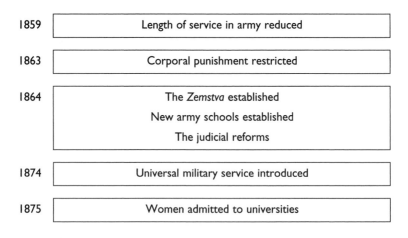

1859	Length of service in army reduced
1863	Corporal punishment restricted
1864	The *Zemstva* established New army schools established The judicial reforms
1874	Universal military service introduced
1875	Women admitted to universities

Working on Chapter 5

This chapter contains many details – valuable details, since no self-respecting student is satisfied with mere generalisations. On the other hand, do not allow yourself to be swamped by precise facts. Look for *patterns* in all of Alexander's reforms; examine the Tsar's motives; and judge whether the reforms were radical enough to meet Russia's needs. For the last issue, much depends on our perspective. Many recent scholars, aware of the failure of Gorbachev's attempt at 'reform from above' in the 1980s, now see Alexander II's reforms in a more sympathetic light. But avoid reaching final decisions until you have read the next chapter, on the response to the reforms.

Answering structured and essay questions on Chapter 5

First, tackle the following straightforward structured question:

a) Describe one social, one economic and one political problem faced by Alexander II. (*6 marks*)
b) How did Alexander try to deal with these problems? (*10 marks*)
c) To what extent was Alexander successful in dealing with these problems? (*14 marks*)

Notice how the less purely factual and the more evaluative the questions become, the higher the marks are. But do not think the amount you write must vary in proportion with the marks. You are rewarded for the quality of your ideas, and these take time to think through.

You will need to use the information in this chapter together with the information in the last chapter to answer general questions on Alexander's domestic policy. Carefully consider the following questions:

1. Why did Alexander II introduce so much reform?
2. Whose needs were met by the reforms of Alexander II?
3. How far were the domestic reforms of Alexander II mere 'window-dressing by a Tsar whose main intention was to prevent more radical change'?

Divide each of these titles into smaller, more manageable sub-questions. The most complicated question becomes relatively simple if broken down into sections.

Source-based questions on Chapter 5

1. Local government and legal reforms
Carefully read the extracts from Valuev on page 75 and from Wallace on page 76; and then also those from the Tsar on page 77 and Wallace on page 77. Answer the following questions:

a) What reason does Valuev present for not giving the *zemstva* power over 'Imperial taxes'? (2 marks)
b) What did Wallace find most surprising about the *zemstva*? Explain why he was surprised. (*5 marks*)

c) What hopes does the Tsar express for the judicial reform? (*2 marks*)

d) Does Wallace's second extract suggest that the reform was successful in fulfilling the Tsar's aim of making the courts 'just, merciful and impartial' (page 77, line 8)? Explain your answer. (*3 marks*)

e) What drawbacks do the two extracts from Wallace have as historical evidence? (*5 marks*)

f) Use the extracts, and your own knowledge, to assess the motives behind local government and judicial reform and whether the intentions of the policy-makers were fulfilled. (*13 marks*)

Reactions to Reform

POINTS TO CONSIDER

There is no doubt that Alexander wanted and brought about change. This change was met by progressively increased opposition from a broad range of groups which, for the most part, grew out of the 'intelligentsia'. The key to understanding this process is to grasp the nature of the 'intelligentsia' and to appreciate both why Alexander's reforms failed to satisfy key elements of Russian society and to determine what made these 'key elements' important.

KEY DATES

1861	*Young Russia* first published.
	Series of fires in St Petersburg.
1863	Sunday Schools closed.
1865	Calls for greater powers for the *zemstva*.
1866	Assassination attempt on Alexander II.
1867	Second assassination attempt.
1869	Herzen calls for a 'movement to the people'.
1874	First major *Narodnik* movement.
1876	Second major *Narodnik* movement.
1877	'Land and Liberty' formed.
1877–78	Trial of the '193'.
1878	Vera Zasulich shoots at General Trepov.
1879	Another assassination attempt on Alexander II.
1879	'Land and Liberty' splits – *Narodnya Volya* formed.
1880	Unsuccessful bombing of the Winter Palace.
1881	Alexander II assassinated by *Narodnya Volya*.

1 The Intelligentsia

> **KEY ISSUES** Who were the intelligentsia? What made them so important?

A major problem with the term 'intelligentsia' is that it simply does not translate into English in any straightforward way. The intelligentsia were intellectuals. In France, even in 2002, you can sit down at a café and have the Cuban exile at the next table introduce himself with '*Je suis un intellectuel*'. It is hard to imagine such an event in England. In many ways the intelligentsia were the heirs to the ideals and dreams of the Decembrists. However, they were far from being a single, unified group. They were the product of the debate between the Westernisers and the Slavophiles (see pages 47–8). Many of them took ideas from both groups. They felt that Russia was dreadfully backward in comparison to the west, and they took much of their inspiration from the west. Yet, despite this, they were critical of many western ways. They felt that western society corrupted relations between people by emphasising the materialistic aspects of life, thus degrading the quality of life by introducing artificial and legalistic constraints.

The nature of the intellectuals was crucial to their development. They did not agree with the autocratic values of the state. The populist Lavarov (see page 94) described them as a 'critically thinking minority'. They were therefore necessarily in opposition to the state as it existed. As they were in opposition, they were necessarily divorced from the existing power structure and therefore tended towards absolutes rather than practical realities. Isaiah Berlin argues that the thing which characterised the intelligentsia above all else was their search for absolutes. They were almost fanatical in their quest for 'truth' as they conceived it. They tended to take ideas and carry them to what often appears to the present-day observer to be a ludicrous extreme. To stop short of what was believed to be the logical conclusion was seen as a sign of moral cowardice. They saw this type of compromise as a characteristic of western civilisation to be condemned.

The philosophical circles of the 1850s and 60s involved hundreds rather than thousands. Even the 'Populism' of the 1870s embodied thousands rather than tens of thousands. How then could the intelligentsia be important? They tended to set the tone, and even the agenda, of literate society. It must be remembered just how small the literate, interested body of Russians was at this time. The total circulation of all the major periodicals was a mere 12,000. The vast majority of Russians were still illiterate and therefore did not even have access to philosophical debate. The intelligentsia thus had an influence out of all proportion to their numbers. Their small size was reflected in the size of the revolutionary groups which developed from them in the 1870s. Lack of numbers made them all the more desperate when they faced disillusionment at their failure to politicise the 'masses' and as they came under increasing threat from the authorities. This desperation made them all the more dangerous, as many were prepared to suffer for their convictions.

Perhaps the most famous of the intelligentsia at the beginning of the 1860s were Bakunin, Chernyshevsky and Herzen. Michael Bakunin was almost an anarchist. He began with a crushing attack on the tyranny of dogma over the individual, and ended with a demand that his own dogma of the superiority of the simple peasant be rigidly adhered to. Alexander Herzen was in exile in London, but continued to edit an influential periodical, *The Bell*. He was intent on modernising Russia. For the most part this also meant that he was intent on overthrowing the existing political and social system. Yet on occasion he seemed actively to support the Tsar. Like Bakunkin, he believed in the superiority of the peasant. At first he congratulated 'the Tsar-Liberator' on emancipation. 'Alexander II has done much, very much; his name already stands higher than any of his predecessors.' Within months, however, he was bitterly criticising the same Tsar:

1 Oh, if only my words could reach you, tiller and sufferer of Russian soil ... You still believe in the Tsar and the Bishops ... Don't! The Tsar is on the side of the landowners. They are his kind of people ... Through his phoney emancipation the Emperor has shown himself in his true
5 light to the people ... [and then ordered] shootings and floggings.

Where Bakunin advocated anarchy, Herzen advocated a type of socialism based on the *mir*. Through this means he hoped to avoid the excesses, as he saw them, of capitalism in the west.

N.G. Chernyshevsky was perhaps even more influential. He was a student of revolution who placed his faith in the *narod* (the people). He contributed to *The Contemporary*, the most popular journal amongst the radical intelligentsia. His views are perhaps best summed up in the following passage:

1 Democracy, by its very nature is antithetical to bureaucracy. It requires that every citizen be independent when it comes to his personal affairs, and every village and town, every district free to manage its own affairs. Democracy requires that the administrator be fully accountable to the
5 inhabitants of the constituency with which he is concerned ... Democracy means self-government and implies a federal system.

The key element here is individual freedom. He sought a voluntary association of self-governing units, right down to the village. Chernyshevsky lived inside Russia and was arrested in 1862. Whilst in gaol he wrote *What is to be Done?*, which embodied his ideas for a socialist state. It enjoyed considerable popularity, especially with the young. The long-term significance of this work can be seen from the fact that Lenin took the title for one of his own major works.

This rejection of what actually existed in the west, by the radical intelligentsia, was shared by their more conservative counterparts. The following passages are from Aksakov, a prominent Slavophile, and from Herzen. They both show, from very different standpoints, a similar love of Russia and things Russian, together with a distinct dislike towards what they saw in the west. Addressing the French nation Herzen stated:

Russia will never be protestant [moderate and materialistic]. She will never be mediocre [prosaic and middle class]. Russia will never make a revolution just to get rid of the Tsar and replace him by tsar-representatives, tsar judges, tsar policemen.

Aksakov similarly castigated the west:

> Look at the West! Its nations, having abandoned the path of religious
> and spiritual development, have fallen prey to the impulse of selfish pol-
> itical vanity ... They have created republics, have tinkered with all sorts
> of constitutions and have become spiritually impoverished.

It did not bode well for Russia's future development that representatives, on both the left and the right of the spectrum of informed
thought, could dismiss so thoroughly what had taken place in the
west. The spirit of compromise did not exist. This was of particular
importance because the intelligentsia did not have a practical outlet
for their aspirations. There was no national assembly or forum in
which they could express their ideas. They had nowhere to go. They
were held at a distance from the Tsar and the government of their
country. They thus became frustrated and increasingly disenchanted
with their position. Some practical outlet for their energies might well
have blunted the theoretical edge of the majority of their members.
Without such an outlet, they sought other ways of realising their
objectives.

2 From Intelligentsia to Revolutionaries

> **KEY ISSUES** Why did the intelligentsia become revolutionaries?
> What form did their revolutionary activity take up to 1877?

In May 1862 a number of pamphlets were issued including the very
radical *Young Russia*, which called for wholesale changes in the nature
and make-up of the state. In June a series of fires in St Petersburg
culminated in a major outbreak which destroyed over 2,000 shops. It
was never proved that the fires were started deliberately, but it was
strongly rumoured that either the Poles or the radicals, or both, were
responsible. Whatever their cause, the fires seriously worried both the
authorities and the Tsar.

The publication of leading radical journals was temporarily sus-
pended. A special commission was set up to investigate the supposedly
revolutionary organisations. It was expected to uncover a secret and
pernicious organisation. Its most serious finding, however, was that
the Sunday-school movement was apparently a danger to the state.
The Sunday schools were then duly closed. But the Polish revolt in
1863 led to a growth in nationalist feeling and a decline in radicalism.
Herzen, who took a stand on the side of the Poles, lost much of his
support and readership of *The Bell* fell sharply.

Though the radicals may have been in decline, demands for constitutional change did not end. The *zemstva*, set up in 1864, began to
channel calls for reform. In 1865 the St Petersburg *zemstvo* called for

the establishment of a central *zemstva* office. When this met with little response, they repeated their request more forcibly the next year. The Tsar felt unable to comply with the request, as he explained:

1 And now I suppose that you consider that I refuse to give up any of my
   powers from motives of petty ambition. I give you my imperial word
   that, this very minute, at this very table, I would sign any constitution
   you like, if I felt that this would be for the good of Russia. But I know
5 that, were I to do so today, tomorrow Russia would fall to pieces.

As we can see from his other correspondence, there is every reason to believe that Alexander was sincere in his belief. Given the great changes that had already been introduced, his feeling was perhaps understandable – doubly so, after an attempt was made on his life in 1866. Yet it was not necessarily an accurate belief. Alexander acted according to his best judgement and dissolved the St Petersburg assembly. The most prominent figures were exiled. This did apparently quieten down demands for constitutional change from the *zemstva*. Yet it also missed an opportunity to bring into the decision-making process many who would probably have strongly supported the Tsar. As it was, they were left on the outside with an increasing sense of frustration. This led to many seeking an outlet for their frustration in the radical groups.

The impact of one assassination attempt must have been considerable. But the very next year, in 1867, another attempt was made on Alexander's life. This time it took place in Paris and was carried out by a Pole. Not surprisingly, Alexander felt in need of more security. This gave those who felt that a firmer policy was required their chance. Shuvalov, the new head of the Third Section, became increasingly important to the Tsar and persuaded him to appoint several new ministers. The Tsar began to retreat from public life, encouraged by his growing liaison with Catherine Dolgoruky (see page 97), which increasingly alienated him from many of his circle. It also gave Shuvalov more power. This reactionary force, coupled, as some saw it, with the lack of any major new reforms, led to a gradual growth in revolutionary activity. As yet, however, it was still largely peaceful in form.

a) The Narodniks

In 1869 Herzen sent out an impassioned plea for activists to go out to the people. In 1871 Sergei Nechaev, who had been in Switzerland with Bakunin, returned to St Petersburg. He was dedicated to active revolt, but a scheme to tie other colleagues more closely to him – by persuading them to murder one of their number as a supposed spy – backfired and he was imprisoned. Between 1869 and 1872 a more successful group of young revolutionaries known as the

'Chaikovsky Circle' became established in St Petersburg. This group was dedicated to putting forward propaganda. Its members did not believe that the peasants were yet ready for an uprising. They founded a secret press and began to distribute pamphlets and banned books, pressing forward with the 'to the people' approach called for by Herzen. They were the forerunners of the *Narodnik* (Populist) movement.

The *Narodnik* movement was quite spectacular, both as a movement and in terms of its failure to achieve its aims. The summer of 1874 saw several thousand students and sympathisers descend on the countryside in the first really major 'movement to the people'. They met with very little success. For the most part, the peasants simply could not understand what these strangers from the towns – dressed largely as peasants, which they obviously were not – wanted. When they did understand, they were more likely to denounce them to the authorities than to be converted. Some 800 were arrested, and eventually two groups of 193 and 50 were held for trial.

Undeterred by this setback, the *Narodnik* movement tried again in 1876. This time, however, they dressed as officials or teachers to try to gain the respect and attention of the peasants. But they met with the same result. They then retired to the cities to reconsider their strategy. In 1877 they formed a new organisation – 'Land and Liberty' .

'To all great conquerors' – a painting by Vereschagin from 1871, criticising the inhumanity of the Tsarist regime. (Vereschagin and other painters took their work 'to the people' through public exhibitions.)

3 The Growth of the Revolutionaries

> **KEY ISSUE** Why did revolutionary activity become more violent?

a) Vera Zasulich

So far the revolutionaries had enjoyed remarkably little success. Had it not been for the actions of others, they might have faded into obscurity. There is certainly no apparent reason to suggest that they were about to make significant gains in terms of support. Yet this is what they did. The initial reasons for these gains lie not in the activities of the revolutionaries, but in the activities of the government. Firstly, the government decided to prosecute those held in prison from 1874.

This proved to be a disaster. It gave the revolutionaries exactly what they wanted – nationwide publicity. Two famous trials took place. They were actually called the trial of 'the 50' and the trial of 'the 193'. The second trial lasted from October 1877 to January 1878. The defendants took the opportunity of making long, impassioned and well-reported speeches bitterly criticising the government and the regime. The idealism and integrity of the defendants made a great impression on both the public and the jury. Of the 193 standing trial, 153 were acquitted. Even those who were convicted were given relatively light sentences. It was a grave shock to the Tsar and the government. Worse was to come.

The sentences were announced on 24 January 1878. The next day Vera Zasulich fired a revolver at General Trepov, the Governor of St Petersburg. Trepov had given orders that an imprisoned student be flogged for refusing to salute. Zasulich took matters into her own hands and shot, and seriously wounded, the General. She was duly brought to trial. Zasulich was the daughter of an army officer. She was a member of 'Land and Liberty' but was actually not in favour of unrestricted violence. She argued that she had acted out of a deep and just sense of 'moral outrage'. She made a great impression on both the jury and the public. In April 1878 she was acquitted – against all the evidence.

It was not just the fact that she was acquitted that came as a shock, but the manner of her acquittal. When the verdict was announced, there was tumultuous applause from the spectators, who represented a good cross-section of St Petersburg society. Moreover the large crowds waiting outside prevented her from being rearrested. She was able to slip away to exile in Switzerland. These two cases made the government look both incompetent and, perhaps worse, impotent. It is difficult to overstate the importance of these trials, although those *émigrés* who claimed that without the Zasulich case there would have been no revolution came close to doing so. The outcome of the trial had a major impact both on public opinion and on the actions and attitude of the government.

The government immediately announced that all cases of 'resistance to the authorities, rebellion, assassination or attempts on the lives of officials' would henceforth be dealt with by special courts. Never again would they risk the open courts. Yet the damage had already been done. The revolutionaries were not slow to take advantage of the change in the public mood. In the summer, political prisoners in St Petersburg went on hunger strike. Some of them died. In 'reprisal' for their deaths, General Mezentsev, the head of the Third Section in the city, was killed in broad daylight in the middle of St Petersburg. 'Land and Liberty' issued a pamphlet entitled *A Death for a Death*. What was worse was that Kravchinski, the assassin, made good his escape with little apparent problem. Once again the authorities looked – and indeed were – powerless. Other violent acts followed, including the assassination of Prince Kropotkin, and for the most part the perpetrators escaped.

It was perhaps this fact which worried the government and the Tsar most of all. These revolutionaries would not have escaped so consistently if any significant proportion of the population had been firmly behind the government. However, if not actually behind the revolutionaries, the mass of the people were either apathetic or sympathetic to them. Even some *zemstva* were involved in secret negotiations with 'Land and Liberty' to try to bring pressure to bear to achieve constitutional reform. The Tsar's position was not helped by what was seen as a dismal diplomatic defeat at the Congress of Berlin (see page 122). The public had expected a glorious triumph; they received an ignominious reverse.

In many ways the year 1878 was a watershed. The changes in attitudes and expectations which took place between 1876 and 1879 can clearly be detected in the following extracts from Miliutin's diary:

1 *April 26, 1877* ... Moscow greeted the sovereign, as was to be expected, with indescribable enthusiasm. Despite the drizzling rain, every street right up to the Kremlin Palace was jammed with masses of people ...

July 22, 1878 ... Public opinion in Russia is in an extremely hostile frame
5 of mind toward the government, particularly in Moscow. The Treaty of Berlin arouses almost general displeasure ...

April 20, 1879 ... It must be acknowledged that our entire government structure demands basic reform from top to bottom. The structure of rural self-government, of the *zemstva* ... as well as of institutions on the
10 central and national level – all of them have outlived their time; they should all take on new forms in accordance with the spirit of the great reforms carried out in the sixties. Such a task is beyond the powers of our present statesmen ... The higher echelons of government are intimidated by the impudent displays of socialist propaganda ... and
15 think only of protective police measures ... The disease appears and the

government imposes a quarantine, without undertaking anything aimed at healing the disease itself ... I am convinced that the present men [in government] are powerless, not only to solve the imminent problem, but even to understand it.

It would be difficult to find a clearer insight into the changing atmosphere within Russia at this time. Miliutin, as Minister of War, was at the centre of affairs during this period. At times one can almost feel the despair and frustration of the author. These feelings were to a large degree shared by the Tsar. When told that someone had strongly criticised him he is reported to have replied: 'Strange, I don't remember ever having done him a favour; why then should he hate me? Yes, that is what I have learned from bitter experience; all I have to do to make an enemy is to do them a service.'

b) Catherine Dolgoruky

Alexander was increasingly isolated from official society and even from his son. His liaison with Catherine Dolgoruky was by now public knowledge. From the beginning of their relationship in 1866, it had caused him severe problems. He was old enough to be her father and had known her since she was ten. Critics saw the relationship as indecent and unbecoming. The fact that he stayed faithful to her, had several children by her, and indeed doted on the oldest boy, George, only made matters worse. She and her children were now moved into the Winter Palace to make it easier to protect his life. It was common knowledge that he intended to marry her as soon as the ailing Empress died. The sympathies of society lay firmly with the Empress. Catherine, however, was soon to play a vital part in the final act of the Tsar's reign. She was of liberal persuasion and possessed an acute political mind. She became the Tsar's closest adviser in the last three years of his life.

4 The Final Act

> **KEY ISSUE** Do the events leading up to the final successful assassination of Alexander II support the judgement of 'too little too late' or do they show a complex causal pattern largely beyond the control of any one of the groups involved?

In April 1879, without the consent of 'Land and Liberty', another unsuccessful attempt was made on the Tsar's life. This attempt prompted the break-up of the organisation. It split into two factions: 'The Black Partition Group' and 'The People's Will', *Narodnya Volya*. The former favoured peaceful methods and partition of the black soil provinces amongst the peasants. The latter group favoured terrorist methods.

Narodnya Volya was led by an able and intelligent organiser named Mikhailov. He managed to plant a spy in the Third Section. This enabled him to outmanoeuvre the nation's security police. He even discovered and 'removed' a spy through whom the police had infiltrated his organisation. In September 1879 *Narodnya Volya* formally condemned the Tsar to death and set about implementing its sentence. It was known that the Tsar was to return from the Crimea by train in December. Elaborate plans were made. Three separate bombs were to be exploded. The Tsar missed the first by taking an alternative route. The second failed to explode. The third exploded but under the wrong train. The Tsar escaped injury, but, more significantly, the terrorists escaped capture. Three days later *Narodnya Volya* published a public appeal stating that they would spare the Tsar's life if he would agree to call a Constituent Assembly. The offer was pointedly and predictably ignored. However, the Third Section still had little idea who the leading figures in this secret organisation were.

Mikhailov did not give up. He had managed to infiltrate the Winter Palace itself with a carpenter. Despite the fact that the German government specifically warned that another attempt was imminent and even pointed to infiltration of the Palace, the security police could find nothing. In mid-February 1880 an explosion rocked the Palace. It took place below the dining room. Yet again the Tsar escaped injury, though some 40 Finnish soldiers died. There was virtually no public reaction. Such attempts had become commonplace. The German ambassador noted that 'One is tempted to regard as moribund a social body which fails to react to such a shock'.

The Tsar did react, however, as did those close to him. Catherine encouraged him to try to win back the hearts of the people. Both Valuev and Constantine made proposals for constitutional bodies. These were fiercely opposed by the Tsarevich (Alexander's eldest son) and were not taken up. However, even the Tsarevich realised that something must be done. He proposed that a Supreme Commission be set up to deal with the problems faced by the government. This compromise was agreed. The Tsar appointed General Loris, an intelligent and dynamic man, to head the commission. Loris was stern but of liberal inclination. He would only accept the position on his own terms, which gave him sweeping powers.

Loris immediately replaced a number of ministers. In particular, he brought in Abaza as Minister of Finance. Both Loris and Abaza were known to be in the confidence of Catherine. Loris embarked on a deliberate policy of concessions to 'reasonable' opinion. Political prisoners were released, press restrictions were relaxed, the hated salt tax was removed and the *zemstva* were allowed to express themselves. The policy began to take effect. Then the Empress died in June. After 40 days (the minimum allowed), the Tsar insisted on marrying Catherine Dolgoruky, against all advice. Understandably, this was seen by many as indecent haste, but the affair was soon forgotten by the majority, though not by the Tsarevich, who felt that his mother's memory had been insulted.

As the year 1880 drew to a close, Loris appeared to be succeeding on all counts. A member of *Narodnya Volya* had finally been captured and tricked into revealing many secrets. Numerous arrests followed and the terrorist organisation was reduced to a very few, increasingly desperate, men and women. Plans were laid for a final attempt on the Tsar's life. Then on Friday, 11 March 1881, Zheliabov, the remaining leader of the terrorists, was captured. He refused to answer questions but boasted that his arrest would not prevent the assassination of the Tsar.

Both Loris and Catherine knew that the situation was becoming increasingly dangerous: the terrorists were almost certain to make one last attempt before they were all rounded up. For the past month Catherine had persuaded the Tsar not to attend the Sunday parade. On Saturday, 12 March, Loris visited the Tsar to outline his proposals for constitutional change. These involved the setting up of two special commissions, made up of interested parties including elected representatives, to prepare new legislation covering economic and administrative reform. He also implored the Tsar not to go to the Sunday parade on the morrow.

The next day the Tsar again saw Loris and signed the proposals. Having done so, he went to the parade. He felt he had been failing in his duty to his people by not attending. After the parade he visited Catherine and told her that he had sanctioned Loris's proposals. As he returned to the palace, a bomb was thrown at his carriage. He was unhurt but some cossacks in his escort were seriously injured. The Tsar descended from his carriage, presumably to enquire after their plight. He was met by another bomb that virtually removed both his legs. He was taken back to the palace by his brother Michael to die.

It is one of those strange ironies of fate that the very day when Alexander gave approval to the calling of elected representatives (albeit in a very limited way) to discuss matters of central government – the very thing that had been demanded and resisted for so long – was also the day the terrorists finally succeeded in carrying out their sentence of death upon the Tsar.

5 The Significance of Alexander II

KEY ISSUE What final conclusion should we reach on Alexander?

The majority of historians would agree that Alexander II's period of rule was of great significance. However, agreement can be reached on little else. Was he the 'Tsar-Liberator'? Was he the unwise ruler who opened the floodgates which led to revolution? Was he the leader who had the chance to implement real and effective reform, but lacked the nerve to do so? Was he robbed of success by his assassin, when in sight of his goal? Support can be found for all these views and others besides.

Alexander did implement more far-reaching reforms than any of his predecessors, with the possible exception of Peter the Great. He certainly implemented more than any of his successors. He abolished serfdom and capital punishment. He established equality before the law, an independent judiciary and trial by jury. Both the army and the economy were modernised and revitalised. Bureaucracy and censorship were limited, education and individual freedom were promoted. In short, Russia was transformed from a semi-feudal society into (at the least) what was widely considered to be a modern state. It was an impressive achievement by any standards. In many ways, therefore, he was both a liberator and a constructive reformer.

Did he open the floodgates by forcing too many reforms on a backward nation which could not stand the stresses they entailed? If he did so, it is difficult to envisage how he could have slowed the pace. Emancipation demanded further reforms: the existing system was based largely on serfdom, and with that pillar removed other changes had to take place. For much of his reign, the prevailing opinion of the public was that Alexander did not grant enough reforms. His father had warned him that emancipation meant revolution. Perhaps he was right. Yet it seems unlikely that an ostrich-like approach would have caused the floodwaters to recede. They had surely built up too far to be ignored.

Did Alexander then miss the chance in the early 1860s to grant open democratic government? Should he have instituted greater reform? It does not seem likely that Russia was ready for such a move. Was he robbed of success as he had it in his grasp, by the bomb which killed him? Loris certainly thought that 'one lucky shot' could undo all that he had striven for. This view is perhaps appealing and does contain some truth, but the proposals put forward by Loris, though they would have been a major step forward, might not have been enough to quieten the unrest.

Was it the case then that the situation was not susceptible to any form of solution? Was it too late for a peaceful transformation to be achieved? Had Alexander been a more charismatic figure, had he been able to carry the people with him, it is possible that events might have followed a different course. But he was an autocrat and he did not possess the charisma of some of his predecessors. He was convinced that he had to remain in charge of events if Russia was to avoid revolution. An autocrat's task is a difficult one. The task of a reforming autocrat is the most difficult of all.

Summary Diagram
Reactions to Reform

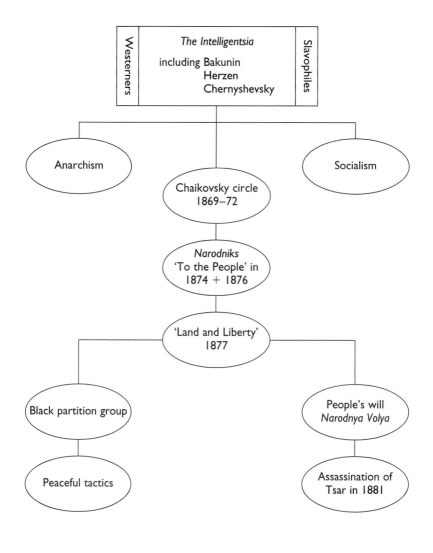

It should be relatively easy to compile a good set of notes on this chapter. Pay particular attention to the final section: here you are urged to make up your own mind on the key issues. The essay questions below should also serve to concentrate your thinking.

Answering essay questions on Chapter 6

This chapter allows you to answer specific questions on the growth of the revolutionary movement, for example:

1. Why did Alexander II's reign end in assassination?
2. Explain the growth of the revolutionary movements during Alexander II's reign.

Avoid the trap of falling into a narrative account, which would guarantee a low grade. Instead, adopt a more analytical approach: this might involve looking at inaction by the government, the action of the government which actually encouraged the growth of extreme revolutionaries, the limited options open to those who sought change in Russian society and the nature and character of Alexander himself. This chapter also builds on the previous two, enabling you now to answer general questions on Alexander II's reign. For example:

3. 'The Tsar Liberator' How valid a description is this of Alexander II?
4. 'Alexander II's reign promised much but delivered little.' Discuss this judgement on Alexander II's reign.

If you grapple with these two questions, you should sort out your own ideas and, in consequence, be confident of tackling any issue on Alexander's vitally important reign.

Source-based questions on Chapter 6

1. Reactions to Reform

Carefully read the four extracts from Bakunin, Chernyshevsky, Herzen and Aksakov given on pages 91–2, and also that from Miliutin's diary on pages 96–7. Answer the following questions:

a) What do the comments of the four writers have in common with each other? (6 marks)
b) In what ways do they differ? (6 marks)
c) How far was the deteriorating situation noted by Miliutin a product of the criticisms of the intelligentsia? (6 marks)
d) Use these extracts, and your own knowledge, to judge whether the Tsar could have done more to stem the criticisms of his regime. (12 marks)

7 Russian Foreign Policy: From Vienna to the Congress of Berlin

POINTS TO CONSIDER

This chapter is about the factors (internal and external) which affected the formation of Russian foreign policy; what Russia's foreign policy sought to achieve; what actions were taken to try to achieve these aims; and what effects these actions actually had in practice. To make sense of these questions it is essential for you to know exactly where Russia was in relation to other countries and which areas outside her own boundaries were of concern to her. (Therefore you should study the map on page 2 and the diagram on page 104 closely, and refer back to them as necessary.) Russia was a European power, but not only a European power. The Eastern Question (the future of the Turkish Empire, particularly in the Balkans) was a major foreign policy issue, as was peace and stability for the rest of Europe. Although Asian interests were less important, they increased in significance as the century progressed.

Russian foreign policy in this period is often divided in terms of the reigns of the three Tsars. This chapter follows that convention both for convenience of study and because there were distinct elements to the foreign policies followed by each of the Tsars. However, there was also a significant degree of continuity between their policies. You should pick out these elements of continuity. But you should also concentrate on why there were differences, what the differences were, the impact they had, and on how far they can be explained by the different emphases given by successive Tsars to Europe, the Eastern Question and Russian interests in Asia.

KEY DATES:

1815	Congress of Vienna, leading to Quadruple Alliance and the Holy Alliance.
1827	Battle of Navarino Bay.
1828	War between Russia and Turkey.
1829	Treaty of Adrianople, ending the war.
1830	Revolution in France, revolts in Belgium and Poland.
1833	Convention of Munchengrätz, between Austria and Russia. Russian fleet sent to protect Constantinople from Mehemet Ali, leading to Treaty of Unkiar-Skelessi.
1840	Treaty of London, guaranteeing integrity of the Ottoman Empire.
1841	Straits Convention.

1848		Revolutions in Europe.
1852		Louis Napoleon became Emperor of France.
1853	**Oct**	Russia and Turkey at war: Crimean War starts.
1854	**Feb**	Britain and France declare war on Russia.
1856		Treaty of Paris.
1867		Alaska was sold to the USA for $7 million.
1875		Revolt of Bosnia and Herzegovina reopens Eastern Question.
1877	**April**	Russia declares war on Turkey.
1878	**March**	Treaty of San Stefano
1879		Congress of Berlin, perceived as defeat in Russia.

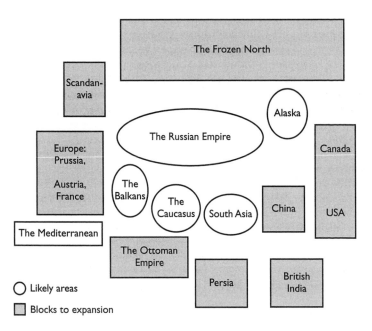

Areas of possible Russian expansion and blocks to expansion.

1 Alexander I After Napoleon

KEY ISSUES What were the key objectives of Russian Foreign Policy? How did events in Europe, the middle east, Asia and inside Russia affect Russian foreign policy between 1815 and 1821.

a) The Holy Alliance

Alexander I wanted a peaceful, stable Europe, just as he wanted peace and stability at home, and he was prepared to compromise in order to achieve this aim. When the Great Powers met at the end of 1814 to determine the shape of post-Napoleonic Europe, they were far from agreed as to what that shape should be. The most difficult problem facing them was Poland. Alexander wanted the complete annexation of the Duchy of Warsaw to Russia, in order to guard his western border. Austria, Britain and France, on the other hand, were so opposed that they actually signed a secret military convention in January 1815 which was designed to deal with possible Russian aggression should a solution not be found.

To the profound embarrassment of the signatories, Napoleon, at the beginning of his famous '100 Days', found a copy of the treaty and sent it to Alexander. It might be supposed that sight of this treaty would have the effect that Napoleon had hoped for – a rift between Russia and the other Great Powers. Yet, for Alexander, there was never any doubt that Napoleon was the greater threat. He made the Austrian leader Metternich aware that he was in possession of a copy of the treaty, but stated that he would never mention it again. The revived threat from Napoleon was the spur needed by the powers to solve their differences. The Polish issue was settled with Alexander gaining most (but not all) of his demands.

After Napoleon's final defeat, at Waterloo, the Great Powers met again, first in Paris, then in Vienna. Apart from the details of the Second Peace of Paris, these meetings had two major outcomes: the Quadruple Alliance and the Holy Alliance. The former was signed by Britain, Austria, Prussia and Russia. It was the foundation of what became known as the Congress System, according to which the Great Powers would meet periodically to discuss issues of mutual concern. Its basis was that the Great Powers had special rights and responsibilities in the maintenance of international order and stability, and that they therefore also had special rights to intervene in the affairs of other states.

The Holy Alliance, on the other hand, was essentially the work of Alexander. It had a very different basis. By its terms, the rulers of Austria, Prussia and Russia resolved

1 both in their administration of their respective states, and in their political relations with every other Government, to take for their sole guide the precepts of that Holy Religion; namely, the precepts of justice, Christian charity and peace ... In consequence their Majesties have
5 agreed on the following articles:

1. Conforming to the word of the Holy Scriptures, which command all men to consider each other as brethren, the three contracting Monarchs will remain united by the bonds of a true and indissoluble

10 fraternity, and considering each other as fellow countrymen, they will on all occasions, and in all places, lend each other aid and assistance; and regarding themselves towards their subjects and armies as fathers of families, they will lead them in the same spirit of fraternity with which they are animated to protect religion, peace and justice.

15 2. In consequence, the sole principle in force, whether between the said Governments or between their subjects, shall be that of doing each other reciprocal service, and of testifying, by unalterable good will, the mutual affection with which they ought to be animated, to consider themselves all as members of one and the same Christian nation, the
20 three Allied Princes looking on themselves as merely delegated by Providence to govern three branches of the one family, namely Austria, Prussia and Russia; thus confessing that the Christian world, of which they and their people form a part, has, in reality, no other Sovereign than Him to whom alone power really belongs, because in Him alone
25 are found all the treasures of love, knowledge and infinite wisdom, that is to say, God, our Divine Saviour, the Word of the Most High, the Word of Life. Their Majesties consequently recommend to their people, with the most tender solicitude, as the sole means of enjoying that peace which arises from a good conscience, and which alone is
30 durable, to strengthen themselves every day more and more in the principles and exercise of the duties which the Divine Saviour has taught to mankind.

3. All the Powers who shall choose solemnly to avow the sacred principles which have dictated the present act, and shall acknowledge how
35 important it is for the happiness of nations, too long agitated, that these truths should henceforth exercise over the destinies of mankind all the influence which belongs to them, will be received with equal ardour and affection into this holy alliance.

Alexander was driven by a religious fervour which seems to have increasingly gripped him after the burning of Moscow by Napoleon in 1812. He believed he was 'the depository of a sacred, holy mission'. He wished to apply to international relations 'the principles of peace, concord and love which are the fruit of religion and Christian morality'. The Holy Alliance was signed by the monarchs of Austria, Prussia and Russia, and afterwards by all the Christian rulers of Europe with the exception of Britain, where the Prince Regent gave the excuse of not being a true monarch. Castlereagh, Britain's Foreign Secretary, dismissed it as 'a sublime piece of mysticism and nonsense', Metternich as a 'high sounding nothing', and from its terms one can see why this view has often been accepted. However, although the Holy Alliance may often have been derided, it was important as a symbol. It was a mark of the autocratic paternalism which was characteristic of the initial signatories in varying degrees. Over the next ten years the Quadruple Alliance was the focal point of international diplomacy, but it was the spirit of the Holy Alliance which came to dominate dealings between the major European powers.

The first full congress of the Great Powers was held at Aix-la-Chapelle in 1818. At Alexander's insistence France was accepted back into the Great Power 'club' and joined what became known as the Quintuple Alliance. Alexander actually wanted to create a 'universal league of sovereigns', but this was rather too much for Metternich and Castlereagh.

The second congress was called in 1820 at Troppau, to deal with some threatening events. Revolutions had occurred in Spain and Naples, the French King's nephew had been murdered, and there had been an attempt to assassinate the British Cabinet. Alexander was convinced that these events were not mere coincidence. This feeling was reinforced by the news of the Semyonovsky mutiny (see page 24). This threat to order in St Petersburg itself, unexpected as it was, seems to have strengthened the Tsar's resolve to oppose any threat to established order in Europe.

The powers reconvened in Laibach in 1821, with Austria and Russia particularly determined to quell the popular revolts in Europe. It was agreed that Austria should help to suppress the revolt in Naples, but no agreement could be reached in the case of the Spanish revolt. As the powers deliberated, news came of the Greek revolt against Turkey, but it was decided to discuss the issue at a later date. One of Alexander's chief advisers was Capodistrias, a Greek who later became the first elected president of Greece. Many in Russia and Greece expected that Alexander would support the Greek revolt. They were to be disappointed. Even when the Patriarch of the Greek Orthodox Church was murdered by the Turks, he stood firm in his condemnation of the rebels. He was convinced that any successful overthrow of established authority outside Russia might fuel further unrest within his Empire.

When the powers met at Verona in 1822 (with Britain now merely on the periphery of the Congress System), Alexander remained true to his stated policies. He offered to supply a Russian army to suppress the Spanish revolt, but was prepared to accept the decision of the other powers, who preferred to see France undertake the task rather than have a Russian army marching across the breadth of Europe. The Congress also condemned the Greek rebels.

It is easy to dismiss the feelings and attitudes of Alexander, and other monarchs of the time, as simply reactionary. However, it is important to remember that they had lived through 20 years of war with revolutionary France, and knew only too well the bloody end of so many French aristocrats in the first years of the Revolution.

b) Policy in the East

While Europe remained, as Alexander wished, relatively stable during this period, Russia's eastern frontiers were turbulent. 50,000 troops were employed in controlling the mountain tribesmen of the Caucasus region who were not finally subdued until 1864. Russian troops also advanced beyond the Caucasus as far as Iran. On the unclaimed Pacific border of North America, Russian fur traders had long been established in what was to become California. These traders were coming under increasing pressure from traders from other nations, especially the USA. Alexander was persuaded to issue an imperial decree granting a monopoly to the fur traders and to back up the decree by sending a warship to Fort Ross, some 50 miles north of San Francisco. However, relations between the USA and Russia were good and a compromise was agreed which acknowledged the rights of existing Russian trading posts, but which stated that the land surrounding them was 'unclaimed'. Possible further Russian expansion was pre-empted by the publication of the Monroe Doctrine in 1824, which effectively claimed that the Americas were of no concern to non-Americans. Yet again Alexander was prepared to compromise in order to maintain peace and stability.

2 Nicholas I to 1848

> **KEY ISSUES** What affected Russia's relationships with the other European powers during this period? Did her overall objectives change?

In terms of his foreign policy Nicholas is often described as 'the *gendarm* [policeman] of Europe'. He earned this title. He felt it was his personal duty to defend Europe against the threat of revolution. He felt that a threat to any legitimate government in Europe was by implication a threat to his own throne. He sought to preserve the Holy Alliance and to maintain Russia's close links with Austria and Prussia. However, Nicholas was not merely another Alexander. To some he appeared rather more brash and direct, to others simply more dynamic. The greater energy that Nicholas displayed in foreign policy can in part be attributed to his early success in this field, and the fact that he came to the throne under the cloud of the Decembrist Revolt (see page 33). Within a short space of time he had achieved what appeared to be two striking foreign policy successes which dispelled much of that cloud.

a) War with Turkey

Against Metternich's wishes, Nicholas concluded an agreement with Britain in 1826 that aimed to put pressure on Turkey to grant Greece autonomy. France joined this agreement in 1827. The Turkish Sultan had employed the help of Mehemet Ali, the Pasha of Egypt, against the Greeks. This had swayed the balance in favour of the Turkish forces, and the Sultan was not inclined to give up what appeared to be certain victory. A combined naval squadron containing French, Russian and British ships was therefore sent to Navarino Bay to blockade the Sultan's fleet and to prevent further troops being landed. It seems likely that all that was intended was to increase the pressure on the Sultan. In fact an engagement took place in which the Sultan's Turkish and Egyptian fleets were almost entirely destroyed. This action, the Battle of Navarino, certainly went further than the British had intended. They now withdrew their pressure on the Sultan. However, the damage had been done. The Sultan was incensed. He expelled all Christians from Constantinople and began to prepare for a Holy War against the infidel, represented, as he saw it, by Russia.

In April 1828 Nicholas declared war on Turkey. The French also played a small part and sent troops to Greece. Little progress was made in the fighting which followed. The Russians were unable to take the strong Turkish fortress of Silistria and had to withdraw at the end of the year to the left bank of the Danube. The next year saw a new Russian commander enjoy a series of decisive victories in which Adrianople was taken and Constantinople itself was threatened. The Sultan hurriedly sought peace, which was agreed at the Treaty of Adrianople in September 1829. Understandably Nicholas exacted favourable terms from the Sultan. Russia gained control of the whole Danube delta, established a protectorate over Moldavia and Wallachia and was granted free passage through the Straits. (This was important for Russia: she needed access to the Mediterranean because her northern ports were closed by ice for part of the year.) Turkey also agreed to grant Greek independence, which took place the following year.

It might appear that Russia gained a great deal from this treaty. Other powers certainly thought so. However, given the fact that Turkey was virtually defenceless and therefore at his mercy, Nicholas's demands might be seen as relatively moderate. Nicholas did not attempt to take more land from Turkey because land was not his main aim. Above all he sought stability, as his brother had done. He felt that it was necessary to maintain Turkey if a wider European conflict was to be avoided, and judged that greater demands might lead to the complete collapse of Turkey, which in turn might engender a wider European conflict over who should control the various parts of the former Turkish Empire.

b) The Convention of Munchengrätz

Nicholas wanted time to implement a number of reforms inside Russia. He deliberately used successful foreign initiatives to improve his popularity at home to give him that time, but would not allow these ventures to threaten the general stability of Europe. Russian armies enjoyed a successful campaign in Persia, where Persian Armenia was brought under Russian control in what was in essence an expansionist war.

1830 saw a change in the relationships between the European powers. In July there was a revolution in France which brought Louis-Philippe to the throne. A revolution in a major power was exactly what Nicholas had sought to prevent, for he feared that any such revolution would spread. In this he was proved correct. In August 1830 the Belgians revolted against the Netherlands, and shortly afterwards Nicholas was faced with a rebellion in Poland. The Belgian crisis came close to provoking a European war. Both Prussia and Russia were strongly inclined to support the 'legitimate' rights of the Netherlands. France sought control of Belgium for herself, and Britain sought to defend Belgian independence as preferable to any one major power controlling the coastline facing her across the Channel. However, none of the powers wanted a return to the destruction which they had endured during the Napoleonic campaigns. Eventually, in November 1831, the five Great Powers agreed to recognise Belgian independence.

These events led Russia, and to a lesser extent Austria and Prussia, to move away from the new regime in France. Nicholas did not view the new regime as legitimate. There was also an increase in tension between Britain and Russia as the gulf between the constitutional and autocratic systems became more clearly defined. Over the next decade this division continued to widen.

In 1833 Metternich engineered the masterly Convention of Munchengrätz between Austria and Russia. The two powers agreed that the Turkish Empire should be maintained if at all possible. The Austrians, at little or no cost to themselves, were given a voice in the future of the Balkans and Turkey. This agreement was followed in 1835 by an agreement between Prussia, Russia and Austria which in effect reaffirmed the determination of the three powers to continue with the Holy Alliance principle of suppressing revolution throughout Europe. Though Munchengrätz was certainly to Austria's advantage, Nicholas also felt that it was to Russia's. He wanted stability and order, and, just as he was revising and implementing a clear legal code inside Russia, he wanted to establish clear binding agreements to cover likely areas of conflict outside Russia.

The following extract is taken from the 'Separate and Secret Articles' of the Convention of Munchengrätz, 18 September 1833:

1 *Article II*: In signing today's public convention, the two Imperial Courts do not exclude from consideration the possibility that, despite their wishes and joint efforts, the present order of things in Turkey may be

overthrown; and it is their intention that if this happens it should not
5 alter the principle of unity in Eastern affairs which today's public convention is designed to consecrate. It is understood therefore that, in
such an eventuality, the two Imperial Courts will act only in concert and
in a perfect spirit of solidarity in all that concerns the establishment of
a new order of things, destined to replace that which now exists, and
10 that they will take precautions in common that the change occurring in
the internal situation of this Empire should not endanger either the
safety of their own States and the rights assured them respectively by
treaties, or the maintenance of the European balance.

In the period up to 1854, relations between Russia, Austria and
Prussia remained consistently friendly, while relations between
Russia, France and Britain varied significantly according to the cur-
rent perceptions of their ambitions and actions with regard to
Turkey. The Eastern Question was, for the most part, the determining
factor.

c) The Eastern Question

In 1833 Nicholas went to the aid of the Sultan to protect Turkey from
the attack of Mehemet Ali. Ali had revolted against the Sultan in 1832
and invaded Syria, and by 1833 was threatening Constantinople. A
Russian fleet, with 10,000 troops, was sent to protect Constantinople.
This had the desired effect of persuading Ali to settle for his gains in
Syria rather than seeking even greater conquests.

Nicholas naturally felt inclined to seek some reward for this action.
He sent Count Orlov to Constantinople with full powers to conclude
a treaty with the Sultan. This became known as the Treaty of Unkiar-
Skelessi. The treaty included little that was actually new in terms of
what Turkey would or would not do, but there were widespread fears
in both Britain and France that whilst Turkey reaffirmed that she
would close the Straits to foreign ships in time of war, there was a
secret agreement that Russian ships would still be allowed free passage. In fact this was not the case. The treaty was essentially a mutual
defence treaty. Russia would provide Turkey 'substantial aid, and the
most efficacious assistance' if called upon, and vice versa.

This was all Nicholas really wanted. He had closed the possible
avenue of attack from the south. He had no desire to rely on the
Sultan's decidedly ineffective troops. Nonetheless, both Britain and
France believed that there was more to the treaty than this. In one
sense they were obviously correct, as Turkey was now more dependent on Russia for her continued existence. They understandably felt
that, to safeguard their own interests, they should do all in their
power to limit Russian influence with the Sultan. Their ambassadors
did all they could to achieve this objective – the British Ambassador
was particularly successful – and a very favourable trade treaty was
signed between Britain and Turkey in 1838.

Russian influence over Turkey may have been strong, yet it certainly did not amount to control. In 1839 the Sultan decided to subdue his troublesome vassal Mehemet Ali once and for all. But the Sultan's troops were again soundly defeated and Mehemet Ali now had a perfectly legitimate reason for attacking Constantinople. Nicholas declined to come directly to the aid of the Turks, as might have been expected under the terms of the Treaty of Unkiar-Skelessi. Instead he sought a meeting of the Great Powers to decide the issue. He wanted an agreed international solution to the problem and, above all, did not wish to become involved in a conflict with any other major European power.

The conference was a particularly astute move. Nicholas had always feared the close alliance of France and Britain. In this conflict France sided with Mehemet Ali while Britain sided with the Sultan. Hence Nicholas, and his chief adviser Nesselrode, saw a way of improving relations with Britain, and at the same time driving a wedge between Britain and France. Nicholas's main aims were to maintain peace and stability in Europe, to prevent the development of a threat to Russia, and thus to allow for uninterrupted progress inside Russia, particularly in the economic sphere.

The following extract is taken from a letter from Nesselrode to Count Pozzo di Borgo in June 1839:

1 The real danger for Europe at large is not in a combat carried on in Syria between the troops of the Sultan and those of the Pasha of Egypt. Neither would there be danger to Europe if the Sultan succeeded in reconquering Syria, as he wishes and hopes to do. The danger would 5 not begin to become serious until, in the event of the fate of arms declaring against the Sultan, the Pasha of Egypt should profit by this advantage to place the safety of Constantinople and the existence of the Ottoman Empire in peril ...

To prevent things reaching such a point, it is of consequence to take 10 measures in time to confine the struggle between the Sultan and Mehemet Ali within certain limits, in order that this struggle may in no case extend itself so as to compromise the safety of the capital of the Ottoman Empire.

With this view, it has appeared to us essential to come to an under-15 standing, frankly, with the Great Powers of Europe who, equally with us, have at heart to prevent the danger which we have just pointed out. Among those Powers Great Britain is incontestably the one that can exercise the greatest influence over the fate of this question, and can co-operate in the most decisive manner in realising the pacific inten-20 tions of our august Master.

The result was the Treaty of London of 1840, by which Austria, Prussia, Russia and Britain jointly guaranteed the 'integrity and independence of the Ottoman Empire in the interests of cementing the peace of Europe'. France was isolated, and realised the dangers of being so isolated. She therefore joined in signing the Straits Convention, also concluded in London, in the following year. This convention did not differ in substance from the treaty of the previous year. Nicholas thus gave up his position as sole protector of the Turks, but gained a closer relationship with Britain. He succeeded in weakening the links between France and Britain which he feared, and gave himself the appearance of a leader whose primary concern was the peace and stability of Europe. The appearance was largely justified.

Nicholas visited Britain in 1844 and had detailed talks with the Prime Minister and the Foreign Secretary. Later in the year he sent Nesselrode to conclude an agreement based on those talks. He was convinced that eventually the Ottoman Empire would collapse. He felt that it should be propped up as long as possible, but that detailed arrangements needed to be made with Austria and Britain for when the collapse came. In what became known as the 'Nesselrode Memorandum', Nesselrode stated that independent action by the two powers should be avoided and that joint action was the best hope for maintaining the peace of Europe. Lord Aberdeen, the British Foreign Secretary, agreed with the points made and wrote the following to Nesselrode at the beginning of 1845: 'Your visit to this country gave me the most sincere pleasure' and 'was attended with no other cause for regret, than that after so long a separation, I should not have been able to enjoy more of your society'. This was the high point of Anglo-Russian cooperation. The problem with Nesselrode's mission was that Nicholas took the agreement to be a permanent, while the British tended to view it as an expression of opinion. The Tsar did not take into account the changing nature and make-up of British politics and British cabinets. This misunderstanding was to contribute to the development of the Crimean War.

3 From 1848 to the Crimean War

> **KEY ISSUES** Why was 1848 a turning point in Nicholas I's reign?
> Who or what was responsible for the Crimean War?

a) The Year of Revolutions

1848 was a clear turning point in Nicholas I's reign. Up till then he appears to have made real progress inside Russia in terms of the economy, education, legal reform and serfdom. He had also helped to maintain order and stability across Europe, and to maintain close links with the majority of the other Great Powers. In one year much of this was swept away. A severe cholera epidemic and the worst crop failure for 30 years would in any case have caused severe internal problems, but 1848 also saw a surge of revolutionary activity sweep across Europe, in what became known as the 'year of revolutions'.

In France a republic was proclaimed and Louis Napoleon, the nephew of Napoleon Bonaparte, became President. Hungary seceded from Austria and set up a liberal government. Bohemia demanded autonomy, the King of Sardinia was forced to grant a constitution and most of the rest of Italy was in revolt. Representatives of all the German states met at Frankfurt and called for a united Germany. Even in Prussia the King was forced to grant a limited constitution. Inside Russia a supposed conspiracy by 'The Petrashevsky Circle' was exposed by the Third Section.

Nicholas was appalled at these threats to established authority. He resolved to take firm action at home and abroad. At first he intended to send an army to the Rhine to patrol the French border, but his advisers persuaded him against such a move, both on grounds of the cost and because they felt that it was more likely to lead to war than to prevent it. Nicholas stated openly that if Prussia became a republic, he would send in troops to restore the monarchy. In cooperation with the Turks he put down the nationalist demands of Moldavia and Wallachia. Most importantly, at Austria's request he sent an army into Hungary to put down the revolt there. This allowed Austria to concentrate on containing unrest in Germany and Italy. He also helped to smooth over the disagreements that had developed between Austria and Prussia during the crisis. Nicholas's firm stand was in no small measure responsible for the lack of success enjoyed by the liberal movements in central Europe. At home he instigated a series of repressive measures designed to stamp out any trace of liberal activity.

Within two years both Russia and Europe appeared to be calm once more. However, Nicholas was deeply affected by the events of 1848. All he had sought so assiduously to preserve had almost been swept away. He became deeply suspicious of any new ideas. In terms of Europe, he was particularly suspicious of the new French ruler, Louis Napoleon. Nicholas had viewed Louis-Philippe's rise to power in France with deep mistrust, and now to have the nephew of Napoleon as President of a French Republic was almost too much to bear.

b) Louis Napoleon

The new French ruler was soon to cause Nicholas problems in a way which he could not have foreseen. In 1852 Louis Napoleon proclaimed himself Emperor of France. Nicholas, already hostile to the new French ruler, refused to acknowledge him as an equal. Louis Napoleon for his part sought to gain prestige at home by success abroad. In a move designed to gain favour with the Catholic establishment in France, he demanded that the Sultan should take the keys to the temple of Bethlehem away from the Orthodox priests and hand them over to Catholic priests. This the Sultan did, although he probably did not understand the possible consequences of such a move.

Nicholas was outraged. It was not merely that the threat came from the upstart Napoleon, but that the threat was to the rights and status of the Orthodox Church. As explained above (pages 9 and 44), the status of the Orthodox Church in Russia was central to the Tsar's position and authority. Orthodoxy was a crucial part of his internal policy. To Nicholas, the handing over of the keys was, in effect, not only a direct insult, but also a threat to the very basis of order and stability in Russia. As the natural protector of the Orthodox Church, Nicholas believed that he had to take firm and effective action. He therefore sent Prince Menshikov to Constantinople to demand that the keys be given back to the Orthodox priests. The Sultan, advised by the western powers, including Britain, refused to do so. Menshikov left Turkey and broke off diplomatic relations with the Sultan.

The following notes were made by Nicholas early in 1853, *before* Menshikov left for Turkey.

What should be our objective?
1. Reparation.
2. Guarantees for the future. What form can they take?
3. Conservation of the position as it used to be. Is this probable?

What are the means of attaining our objective?
1. Negotiations:
(a) By letter
(b) By the sending of an embassy. Advantages and drawbacks.
2. Intimidation by recall of our mission. Drawbacks.
3. By force:
(a) Declaration of war. Drawbacks.
(b) Surprise by occupation of the principalities. Drawbacks.
(c) Surprise attack on Constantinople. Advantages, drawbacks; chances of success.

Probable results:
1. Turkey will give way.
2. She will not give way; destruction of Constantinople.
3. The defeated Turkish army retreats towards Gallipoli or Enos.
4. Occupation of the Dardanelles.
5. The French send a fleet and an expeditionary force. Conflicts with them.

Chances of success; possibility of setbacks:
6. We have the upper hand, Constantinople and the Dardanelles are in our hands, the Turkish army is routed.
7. Fall of the Ottoman Empire.
8. Should we re-establish it and on what conditions?
9. Can we re-establish it with a chance of success?
10. With what should it be replaced?

(a) Keep all its European territory. Impossible.
(b) Keep Constantinople and the Dardanelles – disadvantages.
(c) Constantinople alone – an impossibility.
(d) Division into independent provinces.
(e) Re-establishment of the Byzantine Empire.
(f) Reunion with Greece.
Impossibility of both.
(g) Division between ourselves, Austria, England and France.
(h) What to do with Constantinople?
11.The least bad of all bad solutions.
(a) The principalities and Bulgaria as far as Kistendji to Russia.
(b) Serbia and Bulgaria independent.
(c) The coasts of the Archipelago and the Adriatic to Austria.
(d) Egypt to England: perhaps Cyprus and Rhodes.
(e) Crete to France.
(f) The islands of the Archipelago to Greece.
(g) Constantinople a free city; the Bosphorus Russian garrison; the Dardanelles Austrian garrison.
(h) Complete freedom of trade.
(i) The Turkish Empire in Asia Minor.

Nicholas decided to increase pressure on the Sultan by moving Russian armed forces into the Danubian principalities. He specifically stated that he did not seek war. He wanted 'to have in our hands such a guarantee as will insure the re-establishment of our rights in any case'. The threat did not persuade Turkey to give way, mainly because Britain and France supported the Sultan and sent a combined fleet to the Straits in September 1853. The French largely sought prestige, while the British were convinced that Nicholas sought the complete domination or destruction of the Ottoman Empire. In October, Russia declared war on Turkey and the Russian fleet virtually destroyed a Turkish transport fleet at Sinope. Neither France nor Britain wished to back away from their support for the Sultan. In February 1854 a combined fleet entered the Black Sea, and in March Britain and France declared war on Russia.

c) Crimean War

What was to become the Crimean War had begun. Russia was eventually defeated, largely because her armies proved slightly more incompetent than those of the French and British. There was another important reason for Russian defeat, which was even more hurtful to Nicholas. Austria, whom Nicholas justly felt he had 'saved' in 1848–9, adopted a distinctly threatening posture towards Russia. In June 1854 she demanded that Russia withdraw from the Danubian principalities, and went on to station an army of 100,000 men on the Russian border for the purposes of 'observation'. Nicholas was forced to station much-needed troops on the Austrian border to guard against this threat. The Holy Alliance, on which Nicholas had relied so heavily, was conclusively shown to be defunct.

Nicholas died in the middle of the war in February 1855. It was already obvious that the Russian army of almost one million was unable to defeat soundly an invading force of no more than 100,000. Russian weapons and tactics had made little progress since 1815. The supply system was unable even to maintain an adequate provision of ammunition. The new Tsar, Alexander II, was reluctant to admit defeat. In the end it took a virtual ultimatum by the Austrians in December 1855 (which effectively stated that if the Tsar did not negotiate he would also face Austrian troops) to convince him finally that further conflict would be pointless. The powers met in Paris in February 1856, to conclude a peace treaty.

The terms of the Treaty of Paris were not unduly harsh on Russia. The Black Sea was neutralised (and was to contain no warships of any nation); and the Straits were closed to warships of all nations and opened to commercial shipping, as was the Danube. Russia also had to give up some land to Moldavia. Palmerston, the British Prime Minister, had hoped to deprive Russia of control of Finland, the Caucasus and the Crimea, but the other powers would offer him no support for this policy.

The Crimean War cost nearly half a million casualties. It marked the final demise of the 'Concert of Europe' established in 1815. It also marked the end of the generally accepted view of Russia as the dominant European power. However, its greatest significance was that it made clear, to all but the most reactionary Russians, that a radical and thorough overhaul of Russian society was essential. What the war most certainly did not achieve was a lasting solution to the Eastern Question. Even the more optimistic statesmen in Paris in 1856 did not foresee a lasting peace in this area.

4 Alexander II and Europe

> **KEY ISSUES** What were Alexander's aims in Europe? How far did he fulfil them?

The Treaty of Paris (March 1856) brought a final conclusion to the war. The treaty aimed to protect the Turkish Empire against future pressure from Russia. The loss of part of Bessarabia and the continuation of Turkish suzerainty over Moldavia and Wallachia were galling to the Russians, but the neutralisation of the Black Sea was particularly resented because it prevented Russian naval access to the Mediterranean. Of special interest, given the previous efforts of Nicholas I to establish an agreed international system, was the fact that the treaty was incorporated into 'the public law and system of Europe'.

The disastrous defeat in the Crimea convinced Alexander II that his chief priorities should be the emancipation of the serfs and a thorough restructuring of the Russian state. He was certain that this was the only way to return Russia to the dominant position she had enjoyed in 1815. His foreign policy was designed at least in part to allow him to do this. Alexander needed success abroad to help deflect internal criticism. He needed to split the alliance between Austria, France and Britain against Russia, to give his reforms time to take effect. He encouraged expansion in Asia, as this would further economic progress.

In Europe Alexander sought initially to win over the French and to encourage Franco-Austrian rivalry. This was in part because Russia had felt particularly betrayed by the Austrian threat in 1855, so shortly after Russia had saved Austria in 1848–9. However, there was a more important reason. Stability in Europe was no longer the main aim of Russian foreign policy. It was far more important for Alexander to drive a wedge between his former adversaries. In this he was eminently successful. As he had hoped, war broke out between France and Austria in 1859. However, this break with traditional Russian foreign policy had consequences far greater than Alexander had foreseen, and which he certainly did not hope for. Garibaldi's rising in Italy excited nationalist fervour in Germany, Hungary, Denmark and, worst of all, Poland. There was also a revolution in Greece. Napoleon's support for the Polish cause in 1863 ended the brief period of Franco-Russian cooperation. Both England and Austria likewise supported the Poles, albeit with words rather than deeds. The only ally Alexander could find was Prussia.

Having put down the Polish revolt, Alexander to some extent withdrew from European affairs for the next eight years to concentrate on domestic reform. He allowed the Prussians to redraw the map of Europe and significantly weaken both Austria and France in the process. He followed a conservative policy of avoiding entanglements and he actively encouraged Balkan Christians to submit to Turkish authority. The complete defeat of France in the Franco-Prussian War of 1870–1 led to a Great Power conference in London in 1871. This meeting allowed Alexander to raise the issue of Black Sea neutrality once more. It was agreed that both Turkey and Russia should be allowed to station naval forces on the Black Sea. Thus by maintaining a relatively neutral and conservative stance, Alexander managed to achieve a significant improvement in Russia's position. However, in reality there was a price. Germany was now without doubt the strongest power in Europe. Alexander was understandably determined to maintain close links with Germany. In so doing he set aside his feelings about Austrian betrayal and joined the *Dreikaiserbund* (Three Emperors' League) of Germany, Austria and Russia in 1873. This was little more than a statement of friendly intent, but it can be seen as marking the official return of Russia as an active force in

European affairs, dedicated to her traditional role of maintaining the existing order.

5 Alexander II and Asia

> **KEY ISSUE** Why did Russia pursue imperialist policies in Asia?

Whilst Alexander pursued a distinctly cautious policy in Europe, Russia followed a policy of sustained expansion in Asia during this period. The distinction between 'Alexander' and 'Russia' here is deliberate. As one contemporary observer commented:

> 1 A positive fever for further conquest raged among our troops – an ail-
> ment to cure which no method of treatment was effective, especially as
> the correctives applied were frequently interspersed with such stimu-
> lants as honours and decorations. Not only the Russian generals but
> 5 even the youngest lieutenants craved after further extension of terri-
> tory, while those of the officers who were entrusted with any sort of
> independent command carried into effect their individual schemes. It
> was, indeed, impossible that such desires should be resisted when by
> gratifying them it was possible for a lieutenant in four years to become
> 10 a general.

Alexander, on the other hand, did not always seem to be fully in favour of an expansionist policy, but it seems likely that his stance was designed to calm the fears of other European powers, rather than springing from any deep-rooted conviction. In any case, expansion was favoured by the military, by two of his closest advisers, Miliutin and Ignatyev, and perhaps most importantly by the demands of the Russian economy which sought new markets and new sources of raw materials.

Russian imperialism assumed its modern form in this period, with significant additions of territory throughout Asia. This imperialism was not merely economic in origin. It also reflected the growth of Pan-Slavism (see page 120) inside Russia and the feeling that, as a centre of civilisation, Russia had a duty to bring the benefits of civilisation to all, including the 'barbarian' tribes of Asia.

Seeking some concrete success to offset the humiliation of the Crimea, Alexander certainly did support the final 'pacification' of the Caucasus, which had seen continued conflict for the previous half century. The renewed campaign began in 1857 and was finally brought to a successful conclusion in 1864, though only after the majority of the indigenous inhabitants had either been killed or been driven to seek refuge in Turkey. The armies which had pacified the Caucasus were then pointed across the Caspian towards Persia and Afghanistan. Russian territorial control was extended steadily over the next 15 years. In Central Asia the three great Khanates of Khiva, Khokand and Bukhara were incorporated into the Russian state during these years.

In the Far East, Russia negotiated the acquisition of the island of Sakhalin from Japan, with whom she also established trading rights. China was persuaded to cede the territory north of the Amur River as well as the area north of Korea on which the naval base of Vladivostok was founded. Russia gave up only one piece of her territory in the east during this period – Alaska. At the time it seemed of little importance. The fur trade in the area was already declining because the numbers of native otters had been drastically reduced. It was at the extreme edge of the Empire, produced little revenue and appeared to have a low potential for revenue in the days before oil was discovered. It was sold to the USA for $7 million in 1867. The sale was a reflection of the very close relations which existed between Russia and the USA, and of Alexander's desire to maintain those relations. Though with the benefit of hindsight this sale may be difficult to understand, the fact that Congress almost refused to agree to the sale because they thought that the price was too high, should help to confirm that many contemporaries thought Russia had the best of the bargain.

6 The Balkans and Pan-Slavism

> **KEY ISSUES** What is Pan-Slavism? Why did Russia fight a war with Turkey in 1877? Why was the war followed by two treaties?

Russia's foreign policy in Europe up to 1870 may be understood largely in terms of conventional diplomacy and interests. However, the problem of the Balkans and the influence of Pan-Slavism did not go away. Pan-Slavism was in part an idealistic movement, but one which had very serious practical implications in that it saw Russia as the natural protector and sponsor of the Slav peoples. It envisaged the development of a federation of the Slavs led by Russia. It was never adopted as an official policy, but it had many powerful supporters in Russia including Ignatyev, the Empress and the heir to the throne. The Pan-Slavs had at least one aim in common with the Orthodox Church: namely the protection of Balkan Christians under Turkish rule.

For the first 20 years of his reign, Alexander II managed to control those forces in Russian society which sought direct action in the Balkans. However, 1875 saw the beginning of the first major crisis in the area since his accession. The Slavs in Bosnia and Herzegovina (see maps on page 123) rose in revolt against Turkish control. The Turks reacted by implementing a policy of ruthless repression. The Pan-Slav movement inside Russia had not created this situation, but it took full advantage of it by stirring up popular indignation against Turkish methods of repression and by providing financial support to the rebels. Sympathy for the rebels also grew rapidly in Serbia. Russia and the other Great Powers felt they had to intervene before the revolt spread.

In May 1876 the Emperors of Germany, Austria and Russia agreed on a solution, outlined in the Berlin Memorandum, which was very favourable to the rebels. Disraeli felt that the Memorandum went too far, and refused to agree to its proposals, which prevented common action by the Great Powers. The revolt then spread to Bulgaria. The Turks reacted with even greater severity. Despite, or perhaps because of, Gladstone's famous speeches about the 'unspeakable Turk', Disraeli continued to refuse to support the break-up of the Turkish Empire in the Balkans. Thus common action by the Great Powers was still prevented. Neither Serbia nor the Pan-Slav movements were influenced by Britain's view of Balkan affairs.

They did not convert all Russians to their way of thinking, but the Pan-Slavs ensured that the 'Bulgarian Atrocities' aroused widespread public indignation in Russia. They also encouraged the Serbians to believe that they could count on active support from Russia if they went to the aid of their 'Slavic brethren' in the Balkans.

In June 1876 Serbia and Montenegro, encouraged by promises of support, declared war on Turkey. Thousands of Russian volunteers were allowed to join the Serbian army amidst a wave of popular pro-Slavic sentiment. However, the Russians and Serbians seemed to find it almost impossible to co-operate and the war went badly for the Serbs. With Russian casualties mounting, Alexander was now in a position where he could not abandon the Slavs to the mercy of Turkey even if he had wanted to. In November the Tsar made a firm speech which spoke of 'our volunteers, many of whom have paid with their blood for the cause of Slavdom'. He stated clearly that if his 'just demands' for the protection of Balkan Christians were not agreed to by Turkey, and the other Great Powers would not support him, then he was quite prepared to act 'independently'.

There followed four months of negotiations between the Great Powers and Turkey which eventually broke down in April 1877. Alexander had wished to avoid war, partly for financial reasons and partly because, since his ill-fated support for Napoleon III, he had sought stability in Europe and generally favoured a cautious and judicious policy. He now carried out his threat to act 'independently', and declared war on Turkey in April 1877. Even then, it seems he hoped that the Turks might back down, but they did not. Alexander still wished to avoid conflict with any of the major powers and stated clearly that his sole aim was 'the amelioration and security of the status of the oppressed Christian population of Turkey', and that he was sure that he was 'acting in accord with the feelings and interests of Europe'.

The war did not go well for Russia, with the Turks providing unexpectedly stiff opposition. But Russian forces eventually forced the Turks to sue for peace at the end of January 1878. The Treaty of San Stefano was finally signed in March of that year. This treaty fulfilled the majority of Pan-Slav aims in the area and also significantly improved Russia's position in the Balkans.

a) Congress of Berlin

Both Britain and Austria felt that Russia had gained too great an advantage from San Stefano and made it clear that it had to be revised. Alexander reluctantly agreed to a meeting of the powers in Berlin. He did so for a number of reasons. First, the war had put great strains on Russia's economy. Second, despite the success of the war, Turkish resistance had revealed that the Russian army was still far from capable of sustaining a major European conflict. Then, in April 1878, Vera Zasulich was acquitted (see page 95) and it appeared that there was a very real threat of revolt inside Russia. Finally, Alexander did not want, and had never wanted, to become embroiled in a major European conflict.

The Congress of Berlin was generally seen as a defeat for Russia, a diplomatic triumph for Britain, and a success for Austria. Russia maintained her gains in Asia, but the Balkan settlement was rearranged in a way which was far more acceptable to Austria and Britain, both of whom had feared undue Russian influence in the region. In particu-

Russian soldiers before Pleuna – the Russian siege succeeded in December 1877, but only after six months of fighting and the loss of 26,000 Russians.

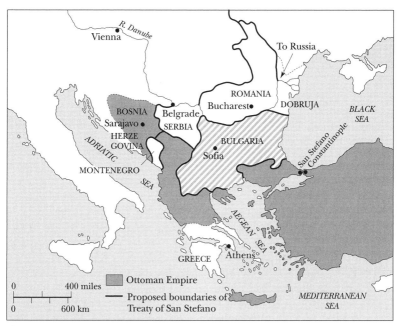

After San Stefano

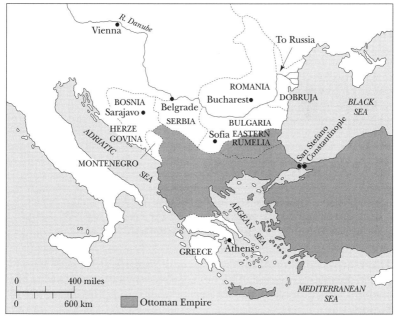

After the Congress of Berlin

lar, Turkish frontiers were redrawn to make them defensible and Bulgaria was significantly reduced in size. Local nationalist feeling was virtually ignored.

In reality the Treaty of Berlin was not a great defeat for Russia. She had recovered control of the mouth of the Danube and had made significant gains in oil rich areas of Asia. The establishment of Bulgaria was still a significant gain and the position of Balkan Christians had been improved. However, inside Russia the Berlin Treaty was seen as a defeat because it was compared to San Stefano rather than the situation in 1876. The Pan-Slavs were outraged and saw the treaty as a betrayal of all they stood for. The Orthodox Church felt it did not go far enough in protecting fellow believers. Russian nationalists saw it as a humiliating diplomatic reverse. The result was to increase the ill-feeling towards Alexander within Russia, which was already running high, and a sustained press campaign against Bismarck and Germany, whom many blamed for the results of the Congress of Berlin. This press campaign itself was partly responsible for the cooling of relations between Russia and Germany, and the fact that Bismarck concluded a separate treaty with Austria in the following year, 1879.

By 1881 Alexander had achieved many of his foreign policy aims. Russia was clearly once more among the Great Powers of Europe, and was accepted as such, although equally clearly she was no longer the most powerful force in European affairs, that place having been taken by Germany. Russia had made important territorial gains in Asia which had significantly strengthened her economy by giving access to oil and mineral deposits. Alexander had avoided any major European conflict and had strengthened Russia's position in the Balkans. An objective assessment of his achievements might conclude that he had achieved a substantial improvement in Russia's position. However, inside Russia, the majority of his people, whose judgement was of greater importance to the stability of the Empire than that of the rest of Europe, felt that he had failed to achieve the position of eminence and respect in world affairs which was Russia's natural right.

7 Overview, 1815–1881

KEY ISSUES What patterns can be seen in Russian foreign policy over this period? How important were the three Tsars? What was the relationship between foreign and domestic policies?

There are a number of different ways of looking at Russian foreign policy during this period. The table below may help to illustrate the changes which took place in her relations with the other Great Powers.

Russia's Relations with the other Great Powers					
Year	Britain	France	Austria	Prussia	Turkey
1815(Dec)	+	+	+	+	+
1820	*	+	+	+	*
1825	-	+	+	+	*
1826	+	+	+	+	-
1827	+	+	+	+	-
1830	*/-	-	+	+	*
1835	-	-	+	+	+
1840	+	*	+	+	+
1845	+	*	+	+	+
1848	*	-	+	*	*
1850	-	-	+	*	*
1854	WAR	WAR	-	*	WAR
1857–60	*	+	-	*	-
1861–70	*	-	*/-	+	*
1871	*	-	+	+	*
1876–77	-	-	+	+	WAR
1878	-	-	+	+	-

+ = Close   * = Neutral   - = Distant

a) Continuity?

There were consistent threads running through Russian foreign policy in this period. The Tsars naturally favoured the maintenance of established governments, especially the other autocracies and monarchies of Europe. They therefore favoured stability in Europe and were generally opposed to change. This was not only because they were autocrats. It was also because their Empire was racked by internal problems, and so any major conflict was likely to fuel internal unrest and place a huge strain on what was a very fragile economy. In Asia, however, the Tsars generally favoured some form of expansion. This was because Asian expansion presented fewer risks in military terms; offered internal economic advantages via new markets and sources of raw materials; supplied an outlet and training ground for the large standing army; and was viewed in some quarters as a 'civilising mission' thus offering political advantages.

b) The Distinctive Nature of the Tsars' Policies

There were significant variations in policy implementation between the Tsars. After 1815, Alexander I was very much driven by a vision of himself as God's chosen instrument, and, after 1820, by a conviction that all movements for change were a direct threat to the established and proper order, which must therefore be resisted. He sought to establish, largely via the Holy Alliance, an agreed mechanism for dealing with matters of common interest to the crowned heads of Europe.

Nicholas I was more pragmatic, and sought to establish an agreed international code for dealing with such matters, as he did at home with his legal reforms. He also ensured that he was fully involved in all deliberations concerning European affairs, and took a major part in the suppression of the '1848 revolutions' and in limiting their effects.

Alexander II, in order to drive a wedge between Austria and France, abandoned traditional Russian policies and supported French attempts to change the map of Europe between 1857 and 1860. However, French actions resulted in just the type of unrest which his two predecessors had feared, including a revolt in Poland. He then stepped back from European affairs for almost ten years, in the process allowing Germany to redraw the European map. This was not because Russia's interests had changed, or because Alexander had lost interest in Europe, but because he needed time to implement internal reforms and did not feel he could afford to become greatly involved in European affairs. He then attempted to adopt a more traditional policy with regard to Europe. The other significant difference in foreign policy under Alexander II was that Russia adopted a sustained and effective policy of expansion in Asia.

c) Perceptions of Russia

In 1815 Russia was universally seen as the dominant European power. In 1850 she still appeared to be the paramount force in Europe. Yet by 1856 she was very much at the mercy of the other Great Powers. Then, after a period of relative neutrality in the 1860s, Russia once more firmly established herself as a Great Power by 1878.

Yet such brief snapshots only tell part of the story. Appearances here are very significant. How other powers perceived Russian power was crucial in terms of how they reacted to Russia, but these perceptions did not accurately reflect Russia's actual power. In 1815 Russia looked far stronger than she really was. Over the next 40 years, although considerable internal progress was made, she suffered a relative decline compared with the other Great Powers. This was clearly exposed by the Crimean War. Significant internal progress was made in the 25 years after 1856, and Russia was accepted back into the Great Power 'club'. However, the weaknesses exposed by the Turkish war in 1877 showed that she was probably incapable of successfully confronting another major European power. This view is strengthened if her internal problems, both economic and political, between 1877 and 1881 are taken into account.

There were important differences between Russia's power as perceived by other countries, her power as perceived by her own leaders and her real power. This affected what actually took place. Her internal problems, and her actual ability as judged by her rulers, set limits to what she could and did try to accomplish. The Great Powers' perceptions of Russia at times gave her credit for far greater powers and abilities than she actually possessed. This at times allowed her greater influence than was her due. This difference between perception and reality is crucial when assessing the interaction between states at this time.

Summary Diagram
Russian Foreign Policy: From Vienna to the Congress of Berlin

	Relations with the Great Powers	The Eastern Question
	1815 Alexander sets up the Congress System and the Quadruple Alliance. Seeks to annex Poland to protect Russia's Western Border.	
		The Greek Revolt
		1828 Russia declares war on Turkey
A L L T H R E E T S A R S D E S I R E P E A C E / **A N D S T A B I L I T Y I N E U R O P E**	1830 Revolution in France / 1831 Belgian Independence / *Nicholas fails to persuade other powers to prevent these changes*	1833 Treaty of Unkiar-Skelessi / 1839 Nicholas decides not to intervene directly against Mehemet Ali
	1840 Treaty of London	
	1848 The Year of Revolutions (Nicholas helps to quell Austrian revolt but has little success elsewhere)	
	1852 Louis Napoleon becomes Emperor of France	
	1854–6 The Crimean War	
	1856 The Treaty of Paris	
	1857–9 Alexander briefly encourages French destabilisation in Europe	
	1859–70 Alexander avoids entanglements in Europe and expands in Asia	1875 Revolt in Bosnia-Herzegovina 1877 Russia declares war on Turkey 1878 San Stefano
	1870–1 Franco-Prussian War	
	The Congress of Berlin	

Working on Chapter 7

You need to establish what changed and what stayed the same. You need to consider the relative importance of internal and external events in determining Russian foreign policy. You also need to consider whether particular events simply made certain things possible or whether they actively promoted certain outcomes. What other overall issues are important in any assessment of Russian foreign policy over this period? This is the time to formulate your own views, on the basis of the evidence provided by this chapter. As an aid to this, you might consider basic questions, such as 'How successful was the foreign policy of . . .', considering each of the three Tsars in turn. Then consider the successes/failures of Russian foreign policy over the whole of the 1815–81 period.

Source-based questions on Chapter 7

1. Views of Russian Foreign Policy

Look carefully at the extracts from the Holy Alliance on pages 105–6, from the Convention of Munchengrätz on pages 110–111, Nesselrode's letter on page 112, Nicholas I's private notes on pages 115–6, and from the contemporary of Alexander II on page 119. Answer the following questions:

a) How well do these sources voice the beliefs of the three Tsars? (5 marks)

b) Do they show significant changes in foreign policy aims over this period? (5 marks)

c) Using these sources, and your own knowledge, explain what factors determined Russian foreign policy in the period from 1815 to 1879. (15 marks)

Glossary

Autocracy traditional Russian system of government in which all power rested in the hands of the Tsar without any theoretical limits.

Boyar traditional and hereditary Russian noble; as a class they were effectively superseded by the system of Ranks instituted by Peter the Great in 1722.

Decembrists a varied group which planned and led the unsuccessful revolt against Nicholas I in December 1825.

Duma elected town assembly/council set up in 1870 as a counterpart to the *zemstva*.

Intelligentsia blanket term covering a wide-ranging group which saw itself as forming an artistic, social and political vanguard in 19th-Century Russia.

Mir village community to which all villagers belonged. It was usually run by a council of elders, who decided how land should be distributed and what and when farming activities should take place.

Narodniks political movement which sought to explain the benefits of a type of socialism to the people, particularly in the countryside.

Zemstva elected councils for local self-government. In 1864 they were set up at the district and provincial level. The nobility dominated these councils, particularly the provincial tier. They were nonetheless generally felt to be a success.

Further Reading

General Books

The most comprehensive account is still that provided by **Hugh Seton-Watson**, *The Russian Empire, 1801–1917* (Clarendon Press, 1988). It is not an easy read, at 800 pages, but it provides a wealth of detail and analysis. Other good wide-ranging accounts are provided by **Richard Pipes**, *Russia under the Old Regime* (Penguin, 1974), which gives a stimulating analysis of the development of Russian society, and **S. Pushkarev**, *The Emergence of Modern Russia, 1801–1917* (Pica Press, 1985). Books which cover a significantly wider period, but which are nevertheless valuable, include **J.N. Westwood**, *Endurance and Endeavour: Russian History 1812–1986* (OUP, 1993); **John Gooding**, *Rulers and Subjects: Government and People in Russia, 1801–1991* (Edward Arnold, 1986); and **David Christian**, *Imperial and Soviet Russia* (Macmillan, 1997).

Biographies

Of volumes with a biographical approach, the following are recommended: **Janet M. Hartley**, *Alexander I* (Longman, 1994); **Alan Palmer**, *Alexander I* (Phoenix, 1997); **W. Bruce Lincoln**, *Nicholas I: Emperor and Autocrat of All the Russias* (Northern Illinois Press, 1989); **W.E. Mosse**, *Alexander II and the Modernization of Russia* (I.B. Tauris, 1992); **Maureen Perrie**, *Alexander II: Emancipation and Reform in Russia* (Historical Association, 1989); and **Walter Moss**, *The Age of Alexander II* (Anthem, 2001).

Other studies

Isaiah Berlin, *Russian Thinkers* (Pelican, 1984), is a stimulating guide to the intelligentsia, while **Peter Gatrell**, *The Tsarist Economy 1850–1917* (Batsford, 1986), is sound and informative. **M. McCauley** and **P. Waldron** (eds), *The Emergence of the Modern Russian State* (Macmillan, 1988), is a collection of documents, with an excellent introduction by the editors. **G. Vernadsky** (ed), *A Sourcebook for Russian History from Early Times to 1917*, vols. 2 and 3 (Yale University Press, 1972) is also extremely valuable. Insights abound in the novels written in the period. A useful starting point is provided by **Ivan Turgenev**, *Fathers and Sons;* **N. Gogol**, *Dead Souls;* and **Maxim Gorky**, *The Lower Depths* (numerous translations exist).

Index

SOLIHULL SIXTH FORM COLLEGE
THE LEARNING CENTRE